MERCY

MERCY

The Incredible Story of
Henry Bergh,
Founder of the ASPCA
and Friend to Animals

Written by
Nancy Furstinger

with illustrations by
Vincent Desjardins

Houghton Mifflin Harcourt
Boston New York

The text of this book is set in Adobe Jenson Pro.
The illustrations were created digitally.
Photo credits on page 171
Library of Congress Cataloging-in-Publication Data
Furstinger, Nancy.
Henry Bergh
written by Nancy Furstinger.
pages cm
ISBN 978-0-544-65031-2
1. Bergh, Henry, 1813–1888 — Juvenile literature.
2. Animal rights activists — United States — Juvenile literature.
3. Animal welfare — United States — Juvenile literature.
I. Title.
HV4764.F87 2016
179'.3092 — dc23
[B]
2015006942

Manufactured in China

SCP 10 9 8 7 6 5 4 3 2 1
4500573591

For my cousin Ann Nist,
who also inherited the empathy gene,
and who champions cats and horses

And for those who harbor humane hearts —
abundant blessings to you

ACKNOWLEDGMENTS

A tip of the top hat to my agent, John Rudolph.

Thanks to insightful copyeditor Alison Kerr Miller
and top assistant Christine Krones.

Applause to all the creative folks at HMH.

Graphic gratitude to illustrator Vincent Desjardins
and designer Rebecca Bond for their fabulous talents.

I couldn't have dreamed up a better animal-loving editor
than Erica Zappy Wainer, who polished my words
without trampling my voice—you're tops in my book!

Mercy to animals means mercy to mankind.
— Henry Bergh

CONTENTS

INTRODUCTION   x

Chapter One
A Privileged Childhood   1

Chapter Two
A Sour Note   10

Chapter Three
Seeds of Change   16

Chapter Four
Bergh's Inspiration   24

Chapter Five
A Voice for the Voiceless   31

Chapter Six
Horse Sense   41

Chapter Seven
Turtles: Animals or Insects?   57

Chapter Eight
Swill Milk and Slaughterhouses   67

Chapter Nine
Compassion for Canines 77

Chapter Ten
"Civilized" Blood Sports 101

Chapter Eleven
Battling Barnum 108

Chapter Twelve
Compassion for Children 120

Chapter Thirteen
The Great Meddler 127

Chapter Fourteen
Into the Future 136

A NOTE FROM THE AUTHOR 154

TIMELINE 156

QUOTE SOURCES 158

BIBLIOGRAPHY 168

PICTURE CREDITS 171

INDEX 173

INTRODUCTION

As the moon rose it illuminated the silhouette of a tall man wearing a top hat and spats, perched like a gargoyle on a rooftop. From his vantage point on the roof, the man scrutinized Sportsmen's Hall on Lower Manhattan's Water Street. He peered down through the skylight at the empty pit where dogs soon would wage vicious battles against each other.

He waited while gamblers staggered to the hall from East River wharfs and sauntered in from Wall Street banks to bet their money. Each time the door opened and a patron paid a quarter to enter, the sudden gusts of air caused cigar smoke to waft up through the open skylight and encircle the man's elegant shoes.

In a few moments, the top fighting dogs in New York City would enter Sportsmen's Hall. They would be paraded around to show off their taut muscles, which resulted from their being forced to run for hours on a spinning turntable, attempting to battle chained dogs just out of reach.

The man watched in silence while spectators jammed the hall, filling every seat in the stadium. According to a reporter for the *New York Tribune,* the arena could hold "250 decent people and 400 indecent ones." A cacophony of voices buzzed below as two enormous bulldogs marched around the ring. Gamblers began betting on which dog would draw the first blood, how long the fight would last, and who would be victorious.

Soon the referee would signal the start of the fight. The two dogs would be released from opposite corners to meet in the middle; then the dogs would rip their opponent apart as handlers spurred them on. The fight would be to the death, or until one dog was so badly wounded that the loser would be tossed to die in a heap a short time later.

Henry Bergh wouldn't let this brutal battle begin. The man on the roof plunged through the skylight and into the middle of the pit, followed by a humane society officer. The men in the audience jeered and taunted the towering man in the top hat for interrupting their "sport."

Unfortunately, the law didn't lock the doors of Sportsmen's Hall that night in 1866. Bergh blundered on the timing of his dramatic entrance. Since he hadn't witnessed the handlers provoking their dogs to fight, he couldn't

Henry Bergh wouldn't let this brutal battle begin.

make the conviction stick in court. Disappointed but with dogged determination to lead a victorious raid, Bergh continued to stake out Sportsmen's Hall. Bergh must have questioned whether he had been a tad too impulsive the first time, but he persevered in his crusade to protect animals from cruelty.

The belief that animals should be treated humanely was a revolutionary concept in the 1860s. It was a turbulent time in America: the Civil War raged between the North and South, slavery was abolished, the Ku Klux Klan formed, and Wyoming became the first state to grant women the right to vote. Not many people were thinking about animals and their rights.

But animals across America needed a champion to protect them from daily cruelty. People considered animals to be property and treated them as commodities to be exploited for profit. Bergh seemed an unlikely animal advocate. He spent his first fifty years as a pampered aristocrat who couldn't decide what he wanted to be when he grew up, and never shared his home with a single animal companion. He once admitted, "I was never especially interested in animals — though I always had a natural feeling of tenderness for creatures that suffer."

Why, then, would Henry Bergh relinquish his creature comforts for the remainder of his life to bust up dangerous dogfights, trudge through bloody slaughter-houses, and confront truckers beating their workhorses? His motivation was simple: Bergh detested cruelty to-ward all creatures — domestic, wild, exotic, or farm. He took aggressive actions to abolish animal suffering wher-ever he encountered it.

Day and night, this millionaire would patrol the streets of Victorian-era Manhattan in a one-man battle against animal abuse. He would be both honored and reviled for his efforts. But Bergh would leave behind a legacy: the American Society for the Prevention of Cruelty to Animals, or ASPCA, the nation's first humane organization.

Chapter One
A PRIVILEGED

CHILDHOOD

ore animals than humans crowded New York City at the turn of the nineteenth century.

Horses were the lifeblood of the city. Nearly 200,000 workhorses plodded down cobblestone streets. They strained to pull carts and wagons towering with goods. Horse-drawn streetcars powered by teams of big workhorses hauled passengers to and from work and errands at all hours, creating a perpetual traffic jam. The horses staggered under the whip to drag double loads along miles of track. They were treated as living machines, and most dropped dead in the streets before their second birthday.

Other animals met an even speedier demise.

Thousands of cattle, pigs, goats, and sheep trotted through muddy streets on their way to slaughterhouses. Some escaped and roamed in feral herds, rooting through garbage. Flocks of poultry crammed into carts arrived at the butcher, where they were plucked alive and plunged into boiling water before being sold as dinner.

Domesticated animals were bred to live short and painful lives as well. Dogs were the "workhorses" of big-city kitchens. Hundreds of dogs ran on hollow wheels called turnspits. Bred for short legs and long bodies, these dogs rotated spits that roasted meat over fires. Their struggle was threefold: to stay awake, to avoid getting scorched, and to resist devouring the roast.

The Lower Manhattan streets stank of manure. They echoed with a cacophony of clomping horseshoes, bellowing, squeals, honks, and barks, making conversation almost impossible.

Into this environment was born a boy who would give a voice to the animals of New York City and beyond.

Henry Bergh was born on August 29, 1813, in his family's home at the intersection of Scammel and Water Streets in Manhattan. He joined a sister, Jane, five, and a

More animals than humans crowded New York City at the turn of the nineteenth century.

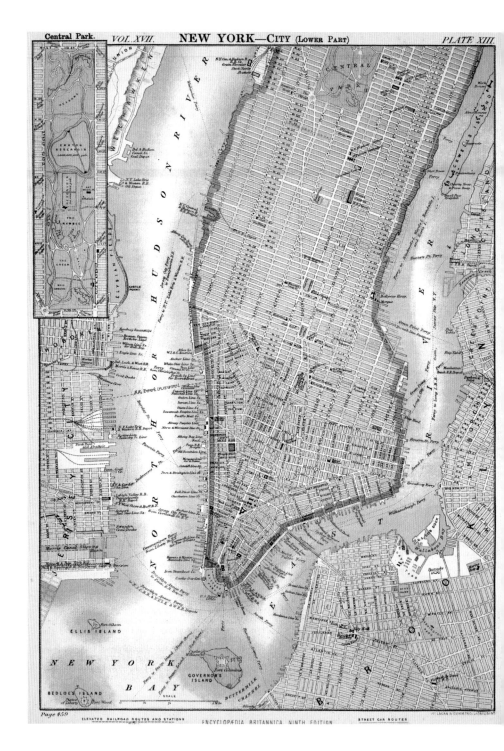

A street map of lower Manhattan in Henry Bergh's time.

brother, Edwin, eleven. The family's two-story frame house was within earshot of the shipyard his father owned.

The East River waterfront rang with the sounds of saws, axes, and hammers. Native Americans once used this waterfront to load their canoes. Now Henry's father, Christian, designed and built sailing ships on the busy seaport.

Unlike many of the 97,000 people living on the lower portion of Manhattan Island, Henry entered the world blessed with privileges. His wealthy ancestors had emigrated from Germany to America in the eighteenth century. Henry's father was born in Rhinebeck, New York, where he first built and sailed small ships on the Hudson River. Later Christian journeyed to Nova Scotia, Canada, spending much of his time on and near the sea. Sailing coursed through his veins like salt water, so it surprised no one when he started designing and building large sailing ships.

When Christian returned to New York, he built U.S. Navy ships for the War of 1812. His brig, the USS *Oneida*, fought the war on the Great Lakes. The U.S. Congress commissioned his most famous ship, the forty-four-gun frigate christened the *President*. This famous vessel was faster than any other afloat, and the British Royal Navy sought to capture the fighting ship, which it accomplished in 1815. The frigate was dismantled in order to discover the secret of its superiority.

The U.S. Navy offered Christian a top position at the Brooklyn Navy Yard, but he declined. Instead, he aspired to build ships under his own name. After marrying Elizabeth Ivers, of Connecticut, Christian set up his own shipbuilding yard at Corlear's Hook, the easternmost point of Manhattan. At that time, New York City had started its transformation from a small seaport to an international city. Upper Manhattan, however, was still mainly farms and rolling countryside.

Christian earned a reputation as the "honestest" man in New York. The hard-working marine architect, who stood out for his unusual height of more than six feet, was as demanding and exacting with his craft as he was with his business associates. The prominent shipbuilder's strong principles extended to his dealings with crew. This prosperous Democrat hired freed black slaves, and insisted on paying them wages identical to those of his white employees.

Elizabeth had a similar reputation. Once, Henry discovered a coin in the street. When he eagerly showed his prize to his mother, she marched him back to the spot of discovery and insisted that he return the coin. Its rightful owner, she explained, might be searching for it.

Henry would inherit his father's sense of justice, his disapproval of owing money to anyone, and his lofty height. From his mother, he would learn kindness and honesty. "I don't suppose I would ever have undertaken this work unless fate had cursed me with a very sensitive nature easily moved at the spectacle of cruelty or injustice," Henry once told a reporter.

Henry, Jane, and Edwin turned the shipyard into a playground. They played among the mast and spars, elbows and ribs, and hemp forests of rigging. They raced along the white sand beach that adjoined the shipyard, and rode the long, rolling waves.

When they tired of the shipyard, the three Bergh children would visit a small zoo nearby, owned by Henry Brevoort, a wealthy landowner. He chained a pet bear in the watermelon patch in the front of his mansion at the corner of Tenth Street and Fifth Avenue. In the back he exhibited deer and tigers, and sold vegetables alongside rare birds.

Henry, Jane, and Edwin turned the shipyard into a playground.

Some families in the Berghs' neighborhood also had pets of a more ordinary kind. Dogs and cats lived in the two- and three-story wooden houses and backyards throughout Lower Manhattan. The Bergh children probably asked their parents for a pet of their own, as many children do. However, the family did not invite any animal companions into their home.

Chapter Two
A SOUR NOTE

When Henry came of age, he might have been expected to work in his father's shipyard. Certainly the elder Bergh anticipated that his son would follow in his footsteps. However, Henry Bergh had little experience in and less desire for the business world. He chose not to toil in the shipyard.

Instead, with his parents' encouragement, he entered Columbia College in New York in 1830 to study law. Henry might have been expected to study hard and graduate like his brother, Edwin, but he did neither.

One of his teachers pegged him as "rich and lazy." Henry preferred playing to studying. The dapper teenager grew a mustache and learned the latest dances instead of his lessons. He wore a fashionable high-cut coat with tails, and snug pants to attend balls. In between dances, he gossiped with his witty friends.

At college, Henry discovered that he needed freedom to pursue what interested him instead of being stifled by others' standards. He dropped out of Columbia. He told his parents, "I'm not going back. I won't be regimented."

Next Henry Bergh followed the footsteps of other wealthy young men of his era: he toured Europe, traveling abroad from 1831 through 1836. He lacked any goals, and spent most of his time sightseeing. He also dabbled in the arts and penned poems and plays, but success — and talent — evaded him. One critic gave his opinion of his plays as "There is positively no merit in them."

When he grew weary of traveling, Bergh returned to New York. He partnered with his brother in 1837 to run their father's shipbuilding business, Bergh & Co.

Bergh met Catherine Matilda Taylor, the daughter of an English architect, at a New Year's Day party in 1839. After a brief courtship, the couple might have been expected to march down the aisle during an elaborate wedding they planned at St. Mark's Episcopal Church. Instead, they eloped on the day of their wedding. Bergh's new bride lamented that she would never wear her wedding gown, but the groom was relieved not to have to follow social convention. The opinions of others never seemed to concern him, so long as they did not hinder his plans.

Bergh and his bride entered the social scene with a vengeance. They and other theater-goers earned the nickname "first nighters" because they frequently attended the premieres of plays and shows not only in New York City, but also in Saratoga Springs and Washington, D.C.

When Bergh's father died in 1843, the three Bergh siblings shut down the shipyard and divided their father's fortune. Henry Bergh's portion of the inheritance was around one million dollars — a princely sum at that time.

Bergh and Catherine, who never had children, traveled between Europe and their impressive house on Fifth Avenue. Theirs was a life of luxury, free of worries and responsibilities.

Bergh continued his writing aspirations abroad. He wrote several more unsuccessful plays. He also kept diaries describing the adventures he and his wife enjoyed during their three-year European tour. Along with the pleasures they experienced came a sour note when both attended their first bullfight in Spain.

Mr. and Mrs. Bergh watched helplessly from the bull-ring in Seville. The crowd cheered and trumpets blared as the first of six bulls entered the arena.

A picador, the horseman who assisted the matador during the first stage of the bullfight, plunged his lances into the bull, piercing the beast's neck. Then three *banderilleros*, the flagmen who performed in the beginning two-thirds of the bullfight, ran toward the bull, causing him to charge. They stabbed the bull with decorated wooden sticks, inserting the spikes over the bull's horns into his neck muscle.

The bull, reacting in agony, gored the horses that his tormentors rode. Finally, the star bullfighter, the matador, began his dance with death, using a crimson cape and curved killing sword. When the matador finished torturing and taunting the bull, he killed the creature by plunging his sword up to the hilt deep between the shoulder blades.

The first of six fights had ended. The crowd waved white handkerchiefs, encouraging the bullfight president to award the matador the bull's ears, along with the tail and a hoof. Then the matador flung his bloody trophies into the crowd, which reacted by tossing flowers into the arena.

Mr. and Mrs. Bergh watched helplessly from the bullring in Seville.

After witnessing this brutal bloodbath in 1848, Bergh wrote in his travel diary, "About 25 horses and 8 bulls were destroyed today, and one of the picadors was carried off the field badly hurt. But one's sympathies are not with the men, for they have reason, know their danger, and are the inventors of this scene, and therefore richly merit death in any shape. It would doubtless serve the cause of humanity if a score of them were killed."

His reaction was far removed from that of the enthusiastically cheering crowd. "Never before has a similar degree of disgust been experienced by us, or such hearty contempt for a people calling themselves civilized and at the same time Christians," he penned.

Bergh's tirade in his travel diary marked the first time he raged against cruelty toward animals.

Chapter Three
SEEDS OF CHANGE

In 1850, Bergh and Catherine sailed home to their Fifth Avenue house and jumped back into the social whirl.

The first nighters resumed attending the theater. Bergh, however, wasn't content to applaud from the sidelines. The persistent playwright used his social connections to stage one of the dozen plays he had written. Critics ruthlessly panned his play, a comedy. It appeared that humor was not Bergh's specialty.

Bergh, ego wounded, bitterly complained to a publisher about a particularly bleak review. "Oh," the man responded, "don't worry if they say something unpleasant about you or your work. The time to get distressed is when they say *nothing* about you." The would-be writer would have reason to remember these words in the future.

Politics also absorbed Bergh. He joined the abolitionists, members of a political movement determined to make slavery illegal. Bergh supported and traveled in the same social circle as Senator William H. Seward, an outspoken opponent of slavery whose frankness would cost him the Republican presidential nomination in 1860.

When Abraham Lincoln was elected president in 1860, he offered Seward the post of secretary of state. After joining President Lincoln's cabinet, Seward helped Bergh get a diplomatic post in Russia. In 1863, President Lincoln named Bergh secretary of the American Legation in St. Petersburg at the court of the Russian czar Alexander II. In his new post, Bergh was paid $1,800 per year to assist Cassius Marcellus Clay, conducting the American ambassador's diplomatic correspondence.

The Berghs enjoyed all the perks the new job provided. They moved in Russian high society, sailing on the czar's private yacht and traveling around St. Petersburg in a carriage with their own personal driver. The gold braiding adorning his diplomat's uniform signaled Bergh's noble rank in Russia.

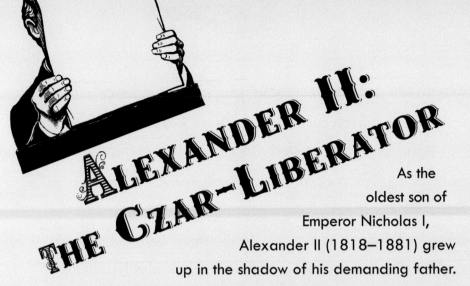

ALEXANDER II: THE CZAR-LIBERATOR

As the oldest son of Emperor Nicholas I, Alexander II (1818–1881) grew up in the shadow of his demanding father. A Russian poet tutored Alexander, but he also had to endure strict military training. Like Bergh, the future czar was a lazy student.

Imperial Russia was in the midst of great change when the Berghs sailed to St. Petersburg in 1863. Alexander had ascended the throne in 1855 upon the death of his father. Five years later, he issued his 1861 Emancipation Manifesto to free twenty-three million serfs from their bondage to Russian landowners.

The landowners objected to this revolutionary reform. It meant that 85 percent of Russia's land would be transferred to the peasants. Alexander became known as the Czar-Liberator. He persevered despite opposition. Freeing the serfs would prevent them from revolting, the czar believed. "It is better to abolish serfdom from above than to wait for the time when it will begin to abolish itself from below," he told landowners.

The manifesto sounded good on paper. In reality, it did not achieve Alexander's goal. Although the serfs attained freedom and were allowed to buy land assigned to them from their previous owners' estates, their landlords retained control of the most fertile 15 percent of farmland. Most of the remaining land was overpriced, and the majority of peasants could not afford the cost. They were issued a loan by the government, repayable at 6 percent over forty-nine years. Millions of newly freed peasants spiraled into debt and poverty.

Alexander continued to introduce other reforms. He set up local assemblies called *zemstvos* designed to help peasants with education, medical care, road maintenance, and farming methods.

Around the same time, social and political upheaval was also occurring in America. President Abraham Lincoln issued the Emancipation Proclamation in 1863. It freed more than three million African American slaves in the ten states that had seceded from the Union. In 1865, the Thirteenth Amendment of the U.S. Constitution abolished slavery throughout the nation.

Some anti-government groups in Russia called for the democracy and freedom of expression that Americans enjoyed. However, Alexander was still convinced that he held unlimited power as a ruler.

Revolutionaries attempted to kill the czar. Dramatic assassination attempts to shoot Alexander, derail his train, and blow up the dining hall at the Winter Palace all failed. Finally a plan to bomb his carriage was implemented, and although the first bomb missed its target, Alexander left his carriage to check on wounded Cossacks and was instantly killed by another bomb blast. Ironically, on the day of his death, Czar Alexander had signed a document that would have led to constitutional reform. Alexander's son, the new czar, immediately destroyed his father's proposal and announced that he had no intention of limiting the power he had inherited.

But Bergh found his official duties as tedious as he'd found his college courses. He often escaped the court to explore the city. One day as his coachman drove Bergh through the streets of St. Petersburg, he spied a Russian peasant viciously beating his horse around the neck with a heavy stick. The horse was struggling to pull the *droshky* — a four-wheeled open carriage — but due to an injured foreleg he could not move quickly enough to suit the peasant.

Unconcerned, other witnesses hurried past. After all, in 1863, Russian peasants themselves were commonly whipped in the streets.

Bergh, however, became outraged. "Even though I could see that it was only a horse being cruelly whipped,

I still heard the cries as if they were the suffering of a tortured human. This burned like a brand in my soul . . . I gazed at that dumb brute, whose skin was covered with cuts from the whip."

He asked his elegantly attired coachman to halt their carriage. Then he roared that the *droshky* driver should stop beating his horse. "Tell that oaf if he doesn't stop I'll get down there and whip him!" The coachman translated and the astonished driver dropped his stick.

Surely Bergh had witnessed other carriage horses being whipped and beaten on streets around the world; these events were commonplace in the late 1800s. No one knows what spurred him to intervene on that day. And perhaps this fiery New Yorker experienced an epiphany when he discovered that his words really could have power to halt cruelty.

The abused *droshky* horse haunted Bergh. He later recalled, "I could see the tracks of

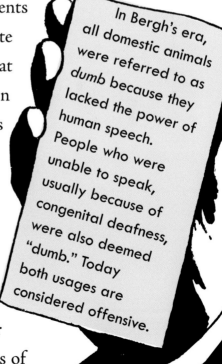

In Bergh's era, all domestic animals were referred to as dumb because they lacked the power of human speech. People who were unable to speak, usually because of congenital deafness, were also deemed "dumb." Today both usages are considered offensive.

Then he roared that the *droshky* driver should stop beating his horse.
"Tell that oaf if he doesn't stop I'll get down there and whip him!"

tears that had been running down his cheeks. These were the same tears that would signal anguish in a tormented and injured child."

This event signaled a new direction for Bergh ... and would change the future for animals back in America. At the age of fifty, this late bloomer had discovered his mission. Now that Bergh knew exactly what he wanted to do, he would devote himself to animal protection, to the exclusion of nearly everything else.

"I made up my mind that when I came home I would prosecute those who persecuted poor dumb beasts and would try to compel justice to the lower animals from whom man derives two-thirds of the benefits he enjoys," Bergh would later tell reporters.

"Mankind is served by animals, and in turn they receive no protection," he lamented. Bergh would later announce to his friends, "At last I have found a way to utilize my gold lace." He would use his rank and wealth to become the father of the animal rights movement.

Bergh resigned his diplomatic post in 1865, only twenty months after starting the job, claiming that the chilly Russian climate was not suitable for him or his wife. Instead of exploiting his social position to stage plays or enter politics, Bergh would champion horses, for starters.

Chapter Four
BERGH'S
INSPIRATION

In Great Britain during the 1820s, a monkey gained fame as a top athlete and notorious dog fighter. Although Jacco Maccacco weighed only twelve pounds, this gibbon fought dogs twice his size.

Advertisements announced that Jacco had "fought many battles with some of the first dogs of the day, and has beat them all, and he hereby offers to fight any dog in England of double his own weight."

On a match day, handlers would lower the monkey's cage into the fighting pit. Then they pounded a steel stake into the ground and attached it to the end of the chain around Jacco's waist before opening the cage door.

Jacco faced his opponent as the bettors slapped down their money. They weren't betting on whether Jacco would win or lose. The gibbon hadn't lost a fight yet. Instead, they wagered how many minutes it would take the undefeated champion to kill the unfortunate canine.

Battles lasted from ninety seconds to three minutes. Jacco would leap upon the dog's back and grab the dog's neck, ripping out the windpipe with his teeth.

On one day in 1822, Jacco fought fourteen dogs. Then he squared off against a dog named Puss, a famed dog fighter and rat killer. During the thirty-minute fight, the gibbon slashed the dog's windpipe as expected. Puss retaliated by ripping off Jacco's lower jaw. Both creatures died in agony.

However, their deaths weren't in vain. They spurred the Irish politician Richard "Humanity Dick" Martin to form the first animal welfare society in the world, what would become known as the Royal Society for the Prevention of Cruelty to Animals (RSPCA).

Martin's story begins in 1822, the same year as the infamous fight in which Jacco perished; that year, Martin drafted the Ill-Treatment of Cattle Bill, known as Martin's Act. King George IV signed off on the measure on July 22. This animal protection law, the first of its kind in the world, made it a crime to "wantonly and cruelly" beat or ill-treat farm animals such as cattle, sheep, mules,

Then Jacco squared off against a dog named Puss, a famed dog fighter and rat killer.

oxen, and horses. Offenders could be fined up to five British pounds (about twenty-five American dollars in 1822). If they did not pay their fine, they could be jailed for up to three months. When asked why he defended the rights of nonhuman animals, Martin retorted, "Sir, an ox cannot hold a pistol!" In addition to Martin's Act, Martin fought to introduce laws banning dogfighting, cockfighting, and bullbaiting, though these battles proved unsuccessful.

Martin lobbied for farm animal rights among the people of London. He enforced his law, yet he showed compassion to those he prosecuted if they were remorseful for their actions. After he witnessed a vendor striking his donkey because the creature scattered vegetables in the street when spooked by a stagecoach, Martin faced the man (along with his abused donkey) in court. The vendor regretted his actions and apologized, so Martin asked the judge to charge the lowest fine. Then Martin chipped in half of the ten-shilling penalty.

In the 1820s, people lacked empathy toward animals. According to an anthropocentric argument, animals existed only to serve humans, who were the universe's most important entity. This viewpoint is embedded in Genesis, the first book of the Bible, where humans are instructed to "have dominion" over all other living creatures.

People looked upon animals as sources of food and labor. Most humans considered other species automatons — incapable of thinking, feeling, or suffering pain. The few who showed compassion toward animals were, like Martin, considered peculiar.

His convictions caused Martin to be the butt of jokes. Members of Parliament interrupted his speeches promoting the ethical treatment of animals with catcalls. Many labeled him a bleeding heart and questioned his sanity. Political cartoons portrayed Martin wearing the ears of a jackass. Newspapers referred to him as "a blustering and blundering blockhead."

Martin persevered. In 1824, two years after the passage of Martin's Act, he joined a group of legislators, clergymen, and other prominent people to form the Society for the Prevention of Cruelty to Animals (SPCA). The society worked to promote kindness and prevent abuse of and cruelty to animals. The SPCA hoped to pass stronger laws protecting a variety of creatures. By the following year, 1825, an impressive sixty-nine out of seventy-one prosecutions by the SPCA had resulted in convictions.

The British royal family provided powerful support for the society from its inception. Queen Victoria sponsored the society, and in 1840 she added the prefix "Royal" to the SPCA.

With the backing of the royal family, the RSPCA amended Martin's Act. Parliament prohibited bear-baiting and badger- and cockfighting in 1833. In 1835, bulls, dogs, and lambs were recognized as "cattle" and therefore protected. In 1854, the use of dogs as "beasts of burden," or draught animals used to pull heavy loads, was prohibited.

As the Berghs sailed back to America after Henry's

resignation, they took a detour to London. Bergh wanted to meet with the Earl of Harrowby, who was serving as president of the RSPCA.

During discussions with the earl, Bergh must have empathized with the ridicule that Humanity Dick had endured. "Before undertaking this labor," Bergh recalled years later, "I recognized the fact that I should be much abused, and ridiculed, and hence it was necessary for me to forget myself completely."

Men of Bergh's class were taught to keep a stiff upper lip in public. To reveal the dreams of their hearts was considered a sign of weakness. The cost of Bergh's quest would include scorn from many in his social group. Bergh foreshadowed his fate: newspapers would dub him "The Great Meddler," a play on Abraham Lincoln's nickname, "The Great Emancipator."

As Bergh headed home across the Atlantic, he pondered how he could form a society similar to the RSPCA so he, too, could stand up against injustice to animals. He had revealed to the Earl of Harrowby that the "long cherished dream of [his] heart" was to encourage "merciful principles." But would Bergh be diligent enough to carry on Humanity Dick's legacy of championing animal rights across the ocean?

Chapter Five
A VOICE FOR THE VOICELESS

O n the evening of February 8, 1866, a storm swept through the streets of New York City. Bergh anxiously paced around the lecture room at the Mercantile Library in Clinton Hall. He peered down at Astor Place, searching to see if someone dared to brave the stormy night and six inches of slush.

Bergh sat and reread his mission statement to start a society similar to the RSPCA.

The undersigned, sensible of the cruelties inflicted upon Dumb Animals by thoughtless and inhuman persons; and desirous of suppressing the same — alike from considerations affecting the moral well being of society, as well as mercy to the brute creation:

consent to become patrons of a Society having in view
the realization of these objects.

He must have wondered whether anyone would venture out this cold evening to attend his lecture, "Statistics Related to the Cruelties Practiced on Animals."

Bergh had contacted his influential friends and acquaintances, outlining his plans to protect animals in the United States. When many responded favorably, Bergh spread the word that he would be giving a public lecture. He hoped to draw on both his diplomatic and dramatic skills to spur change, using Britain's Humanity Dick as his inspiration.

To his relief, many members of the American Geographical and Statistical Society packed Clinton Hall despite the weather. Top leaders in business, government, and the clergy attended. These movers and shakers included the city's mayor, John T. Hoffman, who would later become New York's governor; Alexander T. Stewart, who owned the largest retail store in the world; members of the Rockefeller family; and Archbishop John McCloskey, the first American cardinal.

Bergh told his audience that protecting animals should concern everyone.

Influential Friends

Bergh had friends in high places, and he roused them to sign his "Declaration of the Rights of Animals." Signers included these notable people of the time:

PROMINENT BUSINESSMEN

- **John Jacob Astor, Jr.**—son of the fur trader and real estate investor, who was the wealthiest man in America when he died in 1848 with a $20 million legacy
- **August Belmont**—banker and politician with a lavish lifestyle who financed the Belmont Stakes, a thoroughbred horse race held at Belmont Park in New York
- **Peter Cooper**—industrialist and inventor who founded Cooper Union, a New York City college where students received a tuition-free education
- **George Talbot Olyphant**—president of the Delaware & Hudson Canal Company, who was instrumental in extending the railroad farther south
- **Cornelius Van Schaack Roosevelt** and **James John Roosevelt**—brothers and members of the prominent American business and political family
- **Alexander T. Stewart**—founder of America's first department store, the Marble Palace, on the corner of Broadway and Chambers Street; arrived from Ireland in 1818 nearly penniless and died one of the wealthiest men in the world

PUBLISHING GIANTS

- **William Cullen Bryant**—American Romantic poet and editor of the *New York Evening Post*

- **Horace Greeley**—founder and editor of *New York Tribune,* who unsuccessfully ran against General Ulysses S. Grant for president in 1872
- **James, John, Joseph Wesley, and Fletcher Harper**—four brothers who launched the book and magazine publishing firm Harper & Brothers
- **Frank Leslie**—publisher and illustrator who founded *Frank Leslie's Illustrated Newspaper,* a literary and news publication

POLITICIANS

- **John A. Dix**—secretary of the treasury, governor of New York, and Union major general during the Civil War for whom Fort Dix in New Jersey is named
- **Hamilton Fish**—lawyer and politician who served as governor of New York, U.S. senator, and secretary of state
- **John T. Hoffman**—served as mayor of New York City and twenty-third governor of New York, but his association with Boss Tweed ended his political career

CLERGYMEN

- **Henry Whitney Bellows**—Unitarian minister who planned the United States Sanitary Commission, a soldiers' aid society during the Civil War
- **His Eminence, Archbishop John McCloskey**—first president of St. John's College in Fordham, became the first American cardinal in 1875
- **The Right Reverend Horatio Potter**—bishop of the Protestant Episcopal Church, who founded the Cathedral of Saint John the Divine in New York City

Bergh told his notable audience that protecting animals should concern everyone. It didn't matter whether a person was rich or poor, a Democrat or a Republican; he or she should be outraged by cruelty to animals.

"This is a matter purely of conscience," he said. "It has no perplexing side issues. It is a moral question in all its aspects. It is a solemn recognition of that greatest attribute of the Almighty — *mercy,* which if suspended in our case but for a single instant would overwhelm and destroy us."

Overnight, Bergh had become a voice for animals, "these mute servants of mankind."

His lecture on animal protection stirred his audience. The February 9 morning edition of the *Sun* reported on Bergh's successful speech. The article quoted his reaction to the bullfight in Spain that fueled the fires of his activism. Bergh recalled a family in attendance who "seemed to receive their most ecstatic throb from the maddening stab of the horned animal."

He paralleled this situation to its American equivalents. Bergh spoke about blood sports, including cockfighting, in which two roosters or gamecocks fight each other to the death while gamblers place bets. He described the abuse of horses pulling streetcars and hungry dogs turning spits of meat outside restaurants. He

protested the horrific treatment of animals in slaughterhouses. He condemned the practice of cramming pipes down the throats of geese to force-feed them so their fatty livers could be sold as *foie gras*. He denounced vivisection, by which scientists conducted experiments on living animals.

"I protest in the name of heaven, public morality, and of this society against these fearful cruelties inflicted on dumb, unresisting creatures confided to the merciful protection of mankind," Bergh wrote in one persuasive letter during a controversy with professors of medical colleges where vivisection was practiced.

According to the *New York Times*, Bergh's goal was "the establishment of a society kindred to that so long in successful operation in London, and in the other cities of Great Britain and Ireland."

His February lecture inspired one hundred prominent social and political leaders to sign Bergh's "Declaration of the Rights of Animals." Among the signers were John Jacob Astor Jr., America's first multimillionaire; Peter Cooper, a manufacturer and philanthropist; Horace Greeley, the *New York Tribune* editor; the publishing Harper brothers; Mayor Hoffman; and the brothers C.V.S. and James J. Roosevelt.

Bergh wrote the Earl of Harrowby, listing the names of those who sponsored his society. These influential people matched the RSPCA's "glittering roster of luminaries," whom Bergh had admired. He wrote, "The social and political rank of these gentlemen in their own country correspond with that of the distinguished men who grace the record of the Parent Institution."

Bergh had ample energy to implement his ideas. He brought his petition to the New York state legislature in Albany. With tremendous persistence, along with his social and political connections, in a few weeks Bergh quickly persuaded politicians to support his future animal protection society. This historic step accelerated the burgeoning animal protection movement.

On April 10, 1866, his American Society for the Prevention of Cruelty to Animals (ASPCA) was incorporated by the legislature of the State of New York. Bergh, nearly fifty-three years old, would serve as its first president.

A mere nine days later, the fledgling ASPCA was given the right to enforce revisions to a new anti-cruelty bill in New York State — the first in America. Bergh was authorized to carry out this law, which strengthened the state's old 1830 anti-cruelty legislation, which was considered inadequate.

The new law, titled "For the More Effectual

Prevention of Cruelty to Animals," made it a crime to mistreat animals in New York. The law gave Bergh and his officers authority to investigate complaints and make arrests. If convicted, perpetrators could receive a $250 fine, up to a year in jail, or both.

That very night, April 19, Bergh pocketed a copy of the new anti-cruelty law and took to the streets. It was a routine he would continue for the remainder of his life.

FOR THE MORE EFFECTUAL PREVENTION OF CRUELTY TO ANIMALS

"Every person who shall, by his act or neglect, maliciously kill, maim, wound, injure, torture, or cruelly beat any horse, mule, cow, cattle, sheep, or other animal belonging to himself or another, shall upon conviction, be adjudged guilty of a misdemeanor."

Chapter Six
HORSE SENSE

 workhorse whinnied in pain as blows rained down upon his back. Other horses clomped past on the busy New York City street, their iron shoes clattering on the cobblestones with a thunderous jangle.

Spectators watched as an elegantly dressed gentleman weaved around the piles of horse manure fouling the street. He wore a spotless Prince Albert frock coat and yellow kid gloves. In his right hand he carried a walking cane that, in a pinch, could be used as a weapon of defense.

Towering above most men, at six feet two inches and topped with a tall silk hat, Bergh stood out from the crowd. An ASPCA badge glinted on his coat, and his waxed mustache drooped in the warm April evening air. Despite his dandy appearance, Bergh never hesitated to get his elegant clothes dirty. He did have moments of vanity, dyeing his hair brown and declaring, "Age is a point I'm very tender upon — I'm never going to be more than forty-five." No matter his age, Bergh never feared physical confrontation. However, the authority and respect that his gold lace had earned him on the streets of St. Petersburg did not transfer to New York.

Bergh's blue-green eyes flashed as he shouted to be heard over the cacophony. He demanded that the trucker stop beating his workhorse. Starting today, April 19, 1866, it was against the law, Bergh explained, patting the pocket of his frock coat where a copy of the brand-new anti-cruelty law was nestled.

"Can't beat my own horse? The devil I can't," the trucker retorted as he continued to strike the helpless horse, who struggled to pull a cart overloaded with coal. The trucker insisted that Bergh was crazy and challenged him to a fistfight. He backed down when Bergh threatened him with arrest.

The very next day, Bergh went back to patrolling the New York streets. He was searching for trouble, and he found it. This time, instead of a beaten horse pulling a cart, he spied a cart crammed with calves. A Brooklyn butcher was transporting the cattle to a slaughterhouse. Transport carts were designed to stack livestock like cordwood, with no provisions for comfort. If the animals' heads dangled over the sides, passing vehicles would squash them, or the cart's wheels would pulverize them like pumpkins.

Bergh observed that the calves' ankles had been tightly bound with rope before they were tossed into the cart. One calf was in danger of getting an eye gouged out as each bump shifted the creature closer to a jagged piece of wood.

Bergh raced blocks after the cart, all the way from Broadway to the Williamsburg Ferry. He triumphantly arrested the butcher and brought him to court. A judge fined the butcher ten dollars. It was the first conviction won by the ASPCA.

Bergh's circle of compassion included all animals, but he always had a special connection to horses. They peppered his speeches. He praised "that noble creature, the horse." And he admired "that generous and faithful servant, the horse." Bergh even pinned his neck scarf with a gold horse head pin.

Unfortunately, horses in the New York City streets did not fare much better than those he had observed in Russia.

In the nineteenth century, before gas engines provided power, horses hauled people. Horse-drawn carriages, cars, vans, and buses crowded city streets, causing New York's earliest traffic jams. In 1832, the world's first horse-drawn street railway started up in New York, running along the New York and Harlem Railroad's Fourth Avenue line. By 1858, these railways transported nearly thirty-five million passengers per year.

Hundreds of teams consisting of two horses struggled to pull overloaded cars along miles of metal track. Impatient drivers whipped horses, urging them to move faster.

One winter afternoon, Bergh created a massive Manhattan traffic jam during a snowstorm. He spotted teams of scrawny railway horses struggling to pull cars designed for twenty-four passengers but overloaded with more than four times that number. Inside the car, passengers were squeezed into every inch of available space. Outside, they clung to steps and dashboard rails.

Bergh observed the teams of horses laboring to fill their lungs and scrambling on icy cobblestones. Passengers yelled and cursed when the horses failed to move the cars forward. Drivers cracked whips to no avail — the

Suddenly Bergh loomed up before the first car, raised his hand, and ordered the car to unload.

scrawny horses simply could not pull their terrible loads to the end of the line.

Suddenly Bergh loomed up before the first car, raised his hand, and ordered the car to unload. He flashed his badge as protesting riders thundered down around him. He tied the horses to hitching posts, threatening the railway drivers with arrest if they attempted to continue.

When enough passengers finally disembarked so that the horses could pull without straining, Bergh let the cars travel forth. He advised the frozen passengers that in the future they should make note of crowding before climbing aboard. He warned everyone that the traffic jams would be endless unless the railways hitched up two teams of two horses per car.

Railway officials complied, not out of compassion but rather out of fear that their profits would plummet. They replaced the teams of two horses with four horses. One president of an eastside railway attempted to have Bergh convicted for obstructing traffic, but was unsuccessful.

For his efforts, some members of the press again chastised Bergh. "Bergh makes himself ridiculous. One is compelled to believe him insane or to conclude that he is a mere seeker after personal notoriety at the expense of public convenience," one newspaper criticized.

Recording History: Newspapers in New York

The first newspaper published in New York was issued November 8, 1725. The *New-York Gazette* was a "small two-page paper, poorly printed, and containing chiefly foreign news from three to six months old, state papers, lists of ships entered and cleared, and a few advertisements."

From that early start, the number of newspapers rapidly rose. From 1725 through 1800, about 137 newspapers were published in New York State, some for only a few editions. Small-town printers issued most of these early American newspapers. Their content reflected the interests of the local communities they served.

By the time Henry Bergh was a teenager, readers in New York State could buy 120 regional newspapers, including 20 published in New York City. Articles focused on social, political, and cultural events.

Soon-to-be famous writers and poets gained their experience writing or working for New York newspapers —these included Walt Whitman, Herman Melville, and Mark Twain. Washington Irving wrote for a paper that Aaron Burr started. Clement Clark Moore's "Account of a Visit from St. Nicholas" and several of Emily Dickinson's poems were published in newspapers anonymously.

Newspaper sales surged in the early 1830s, when new steam-powered presses produced the papers inexpensively. They sold for one cent rather than the customary six cents. This meant that most American citizens could afford to purchase a paper to read the news.

The *Sun* was the first popular penny paper. This daily New York newspaper published crime and human interest stories to attract working-class readers. It also became the most widely circulated paper in the world after publishing the "moon hoax," a series of articles claiming that scientists had discovered life on the moon.

The *Sun's* main rival, the *New York Herald,* published

more news stories than any other New York paper at the time. Reporters gathered news through interviews and by attending art and cultural events. The paper used carrier pigeons and the telegraph to speed along the delivery of information. The *Herald* focused on topics not usually covered in newspapers, such as finance, foreign events, society, and sports. Unlike its rivals, the *Herald* was politically independent and endorsed candidates from various parties.

Other penny papers joined in the competition, including the *New York Tribune* and the *New York Times*. These dailies had higher standards than most one-cent papers. Instead of placing emphasis on the most shocking aspects of current events, they reported the news objectively.

Newspapers continued to multiply in the mid-nineteenth century. By 1865, 373 newspapers rolled off U.S. printing presses each day, with 54 of them published in New York City. They lured readers with blaring headlines, morning and evening editions, and the speedy reporting of news. These papers helped shape New York's identity, fueling discussions about important political and social issues.

The ASPCA president endured the jibes. He also demonstrated that even though reviewers said his plays weren't funny, he did indeed have a sense of humor. One day he spotted a driver whose horse was pulling a cart loaded with a stack of boxes nearly two stories high. A crowd gathered, waiting for the fireworks to fly. But the joke was on Bergh: the boxes were purposely empty. He joined in the crowd's laughter.

Although he had critics, Bergh also had many supporters, among them Louisa May Alcott. The author mentioned him in "Rosa's Tale," her short story featuring a horse who gains the gift of speech for one hour after midnight on Christmas Eve. Rosa describes for a young girl the happiness and heartbreak she suffered at the hands of humans. The bay mare says, "I have often longed to ask why Mr. Bergh does not try to prevent such crowds from piling into those cars; and now I beg you to do what you can to stop such an unmerciful abuse."

Harper's Weekly also sided with Bergh in an editorial titled "Cruelty to Bipeds." The editor noted how passengers were "packed into cars like fish in barrels." The magazine published a poem, "Street-Car Salad," about the problem of overcrowding:

Never full! pack 'em in!
Move up, fat man, squeeze in, thin.
Thirty seated, forty standing,
A dozen more on either landing.

Besides the ones pulling streetcars, other work-horses strained to pull butcher carts and drays — large, low carts designed for heavy loads. Urban horses powered every wheel, yet were exploited and abused during their brief life span. These hard-working animals were literally worked to death. The majority collapsed and died on city streets before reaching their second birthday. Others broke their legs when they slid on slippery cobblestones, and had to be destroyed. "The horse, what does he get for his prodigious services to us, more than blows, neglect, and starvation," Bergh pondered.

In 1866, the year the ASPCA was founded, the *Atlantic Monthly* described Broadway as congested with "dead horses and vehicular entanglements." Thousands of dead horses also clogged the city's bays and rivers, where they were dumped with the daily trash. Expendable horses and costly horse feed gave rise to the saying "Horses are cheaper than oats."

LOUISA MAY ALCOTT

The author Louisa May Alcott (1832–1888) remains popular today for her children's novels, especially *Little Women,* which has sold millions of copies in more than fifty languages. Alcott was a prolific writer, penning hundreds of works of fiction and nonfiction, poems, dramas, and thrillers.

She started keeping a journal at the age of eight. In its pages she recorded her emotions and the difficulty she had controlling her temper. Alcott and her three sisters grew up in New England, where poverty forced the family to move thirty times. Although she never went to school, Alcott and her family were surrounded by intellectuals such as the great American thinkers and writers Ralph Waldo Emerson and Henry David Thoreau.

Alcott dreamed of alleviating her family's financial woes. However, she struggled to earn a living through a variety of jobs as governess, teacher, and servant. She became determined to "turn [her] brains into money by stories." She sold her first story, written when she was fifteen, for five dollars, but pronounced it "great rubbish." Soon Alcott's writings appeared in publications under different pen names.

Her stint as a Civil War nurse inspired Alcott to write *Hospital Sketches.* When this book was published in 1863, it became her first bestseller.

Five years later, the author published *Little Women,* a fictionalized account of growing up with her three sisters. She dashed off the novel in two and a half months, after her publisher recommended that she write a book for girls. It was the last thing Alcott wanted to write. "So I plod away, though I don't enjoy this sort of thing," she wrote in her journal. "Never liked girls or knew many, except my sisters; but our . . . experiences may prove interesting, though I doubt it."

Despite her skepticism, *Little Women* brought Alcott literary acclaim and the fortune she had been seeking. She would later write about this experience in the margin of her journal: "Good joke."

Alcott wrote a steady stream of novels based on her family life, including *Little Men, Eight Cousins,* and *Jo's Boys.* Although her books gave the Alcott family financial independence, the author considered them "moral pap for the young." She proclaimed herself "the goose that laid the golden egg," and continued churning out books.

Alcott found solace in her religion. She was a Unitarian, as were Bergh and other supporters of the ASPCA, including Emerson and the poet Henry Wadsworth Longfellow. This religion encourages its followers to search for meaning in life. Unitarians believe in the power of religion to make a difference in the world; therefore, many are active in social change. Their motto is "Deeds speak louder than words."

Alcott supported a variety of causes. She went door to door campaigning for women's suffrage and encouraging women to register to vote. She taught illiterate immigrants how to read and write. She and her family supported abolition and were conductors on the Underground Railroad, hiding fugitive slaves in their flight to freedom.

Horses who didn't die on the job usually suffered other sad fates. Hundreds were incinerated when the rickety wooden stables that dotted the city burned periodically. Old, sick workhorses who had outlived their usefulness were sold for their skins. Their carcasses were dragged down to the offal dock on West Thirty-Eighth Street. Rendering firms separated the fat from the horses' remains by slow heating. Then these firms transformed the offal, or edible internal organs (brains, heart, liver, and stomach), fat, bones, and hooves into products such as fertilizer, gelatin, and glue.

Bergh chastised a man who disposed of his old horse for a pittance. "The few dollars you might get for him may blister your hands and soul," he wrote. Bergh thought that horses, and other animals, deserved better at the end of their working days. "When that most useful of all man's servants is unfit for further service, it is the duty of good men to mercifully kill them. Prosperity will never come to those who abuse the dumb and speechless of God's creation," he said.

After a deadly horse "plague" struck northern American cities in 1872, the economy ground to a halt. The influenza, which originated in Canada, resulted in the deaths of more than 2,500 horses in New York City. People were forced to transform into beasts of burden, using pushcarts and wheelbarrows to transport the merchandise that was piling up at docks. As the remaining horses recovered, Bergh called for improved treatment of city horses.

The ASPCA president even set up a retirement stable for old carriage horses at his summer estate on the shore of Lake Mahopac, about fifty miles north of New York City. One visitor was astonished when he first spotted Bergh's horses, expecting to see spirited thoroughbreds instead of the bony "great, lean, rawboned beasts," former carriage horses, who greeted him.

Bergh also helped horses survive the mean city streets with a new invention. The ASPCA rolled out a seven-hundred-dollar motorized ambulance designed for ill and injured horses and other large animals. Its movable floor could be cranked out and slid under equine patients. Then they could be driven to a stable and treated by veterinarians. It would be two more years before Bellevue Hospital introduced the first ambulance service for people. The novel sight of a horse ambulance always attracted a crowd of onlookers. A preacher once told Bergh, "That ambulance preaches a better sermon than I can" (about compassion toward animals).

Later, Bergh invented a canvas sling to rescue horses

who had fallen into the river or gotten stuck in mud. This sling would be used to rescue injured horses during World War I.

The ASPCA also introduced drinking troughs for thirsty city horses. Not to leave anyone out, the society later designed a triple drinking fountain: the horse trough, a smaller basin below for dogs and cats, and a faucet on the opposite side with a cup chained beside it for thirsty people.

Chapter Seven

TURTLES: ANIMALS OR INSECTS?

 few months after the ASPCA had formed, Bergh received a tip about a schooner loaded with turtles. He hurried down to the East River wharf. It was time to meddle.

Bergh and his agents tramped up the ramp of the *Active*. They gazed in horror at dozens of green sea turtles upside down on the deck. The creatures struggled to turn upright.

Bergh inquired whether the turtles had received nourishment since their capture in the tropics. Captain Nehemiah Calhoun responded that the turtles had been doused with water. He insisted that Bergh disembark so his crew could load the turtles onto a wagon and deliver them to the Fulton Fish Market.

As deckhands untied the ropes imprisoning the dehydrated and starving turtles, Bergh became increasingly outraged. The turtles' paddle-like flippers, which enable them to gracefully swim through the sea, had been pierced with a pointy tool. Then a single rope had been woven through the wounds, tying together all the turtles in a deadly web. Bergh ordered the captain and crew arrested. "If I had it my way," he said, "I'd arrange it so none of you could move either."

However, when the case went to trial, the president of the ASPCA was shocked when defense attorneys argued that turtles were not animals, and therefore no laws had been broken.

Green sea turtles are cold-blooded reptiles whose existence dates back to the age of the dinosaurs. Everything about them is big. In the wild, they live more than eighty years, grow up to five feet, and weigh up to seven hundred pounds.

In the 1800s, the demand for green sea turtle products ensured a thriving trade. Ship crews captured turtles and slaughtered them for their meat, which was sliced into steaks and diced for soups. Their heart-shaped carapaces,

Bergh and his agents gazed in horror at dozens of green sea turtles upside down on the deck.

or shells, were carved into combs and other jewelry. Their skins were tanned and turned into leather trinkets.

Bergh couldn't halt the hunt for green sea turtles that took place in the Atlantic, Pacific, and Indian Oceans — it was simply too big a job for just one man to undertake — but he strove to extend protection to these animals during their long journeys aboard ships. During the 1866 "turtle trial," as it became known, Bergh battled over the scientific classification of turtles.

When the council for Captain Calhoun and his crew argued that turtles should not be classified as animals, Bergh brought forth the counterargument that there were only three kingdoms in nature. Since turtles weren't vegetables or minerals, by the process of elimination, they must be animals.

Bergh obtained a letter from Professor Louis Agassiz, a famous Harvard zoologist. The professor agreed that turtles were sensitive to pain.

Agassiz reasoned that when these large creatures are flipped upside down, they endure painful pressure on their organs. "To say that the turtle does not suffer when dragged from its natural haunts and tied so it cannot move is absurd," the professor wrote.

As the trial dragged on for nine days, it attracted plenty of publicity. People packed the courtroom. Newspapers devoted inches of ink to covering the case, and to ridiculing Bergh. The ASPCA president took the taunts in stride, believing that there was no such thing as bad publicity.

Bergh later lectured about how he was grateful to a writer with the *New York Herald* who wrote six columns covering the turtle trial. The reporter labeled Bergh the "Moses of the [animal rights] movement" and published a satire featuring talking animals who gathered at Union Square to express their appreciation of his work.

"I have always felt grateful, for [the reporter's] ridicule awakened the public from its apathy. Next day one million people understood my purpose and in a week, twenty million knew there was a society for the defense of inferior animals," Bergh rejoiced. The exposure was worth enduring cartoons showing him being hugged by a turtle's flippers.

A local restaurant even displayed a live turtle atop a pillow. Above it was this sign: "Having no desire to wound the feelings of any member of the American Society for the Prevention of Cruelty to Animals, or of its President,

Henry Bergh, we have done what we could for the comfort of this poor turtle during the few remaining days of his life. He will be served in soups and steaks on Thursday and Friday. Members of the aforesaid Society and others are invited to come and do justice to his memory."

In the end, the judge acquitted the captain and crew on the grounds that the turtle was "not an animal within the meaning of the law." In his ruling, the judge classified turtles as insects.

Bergh lost the turtle trial — one of his few unsuccessful attempts at animal welfare. (The ASPCA would continue to have an outstanding success ratio, obtaining convictions in more than 90 percent of all cases pursued in court.) However, the media attention gave the ASPCA the spotlight it desired. Donations ranging from a single penny to a thousand dollars poured in, and its membership grew.

Bergh always wrote letters to children who had mailed tiny donations, thanking them for both their support and their compassion for animals. He responded to one young girl who sent in twenty-five cents, writing, "As for your gift . . . in as much as it represents your sympathy with the cause of humanity, and your affectionate

THREE KINGDOMS

The Swedish botanist Carl Linnaeus (1707–1778) sorted living things into categories. He distinguished two kingdoms of living things—the animal kingdom and the vegetable kingdom—and a separate third kingdom, the mineral kingdom. The animal kingdom can be divided into two basic groups. Vertebrates (animals with a backbone) include amphibians, birds, fish, mammals, and reptiles. Invertebrates (animals who lack a backbone) include annelid worms, arachnids, coelenterates, crustaceans, echinoderms, flatworms, insects, mollusks, myriapods, and protozoa. Green sea turtles belong to the reptile class, which includes seven species of sea turtles.

tenderness towards dumb animals, I appreciate it just as much as though it were thousands of dollars."

Five years after the "turtle trial," the ASPCA would snag its first major donor. This donor had, ironically, amassed a fortune by ensnaring animals for their pelts, which he traded with Native Americans as a French trapper.

Louis Bonard was on his deathbed in the winter of 1871 when he noticed cartoons of Bergh as an object of ridicule. A hospital attendant described the ASPCA's mission and how lack of funds was hindering it. Bonard insisted that the attendant summon Bergh. The trapper wanted to make amends for his past. He also believed in reincarnation and was convinced that after his death, his soul would be reborn in the body of a carriage horse.

Bonard told Bergh he would be leaving the ASPCA his money and property. (Bonard's relatives would contest his will, claiming that he had been insane and citing his belief in reincarnation as evidence, but the court upheld his will.) A few days later the president was amazed to discover that Bonard's estate totaled around $150,000 (nearly $3 million in today's money). This enabled the ASPCA to move out of its cramped attic headquarters in a rented building. The society purchased a four-story building at the corner of Fourth Avenue and Twenty-Second Street.

A drinking fountain for animals and an iron horse graced the front of the headquarters. The first floor contained the ASPCA's two horse ambulances along with Bergh's "Chamber of Horrors." Here, visitors could examine instruments of animal torture such as bloody bit burrs, metal mouthpieces with spikes that had been used to grab the inside of coach horses' cheeks to control them. Also on display was a former piece of court evidence: a stuffed bulldog mutilated by wounds, silently demonstrating the evils of dogfighting.

Bergh oversaw the ASPCA and its staff of three from his second-floor office in the new headquarters. While membership rose after the turtle trial, so did reports of animal abuse: injured horses forced to work, continued dog- and cockfighting, starving cattle, and more. Bergh used some of the donations to hire agents who would investigate whether these complaints were valid. He paid them a weekly salary ranging from ten to sixteen dollars.

Bergh himself accepted no salary. "If I were paid a large salary, or perhaps any salary, I should lose that enthusiasm which has been my strength and safeguard," he told a reporter for the literary magazine *Scribner's Monthly*.

Even though Bergh's Men, as they were called, patrolled the streets, the ASPCA president insisted on sharing the action with his agents. In one incident, he demanded a passenger car driver replace his exhausted horses, who were struggling to pull 20,000 pounds up a slope, with a new team. The driver shook his fist at the tall man in the top hat. Bergh might have been a gentleman, but he wasn't afraid to fight for his cause using both his courage and physical strength. He seized the driver by his shoulder, spun him around, and flung him headfirst into a snow pile. Then he had him arrested and hauled off to court.

Chapter Eight

SWILL MILK AND SLAUGHTERHOUSES

Bergh stepped into the Brooklyn stable. An awful stench made him reach for his handkerchief. It was milking time, and cows crammed into narrow, unventilated stalls mooed feebly.

Slings supported cows who were too weak to stand. Their troughs contained a toxic swill — a mash left over after distilling grains to make alcohol — that gave the barn a barroom aroma.

The dairy owner, like most, had discovered a cheap way to feed his herd. His cows didn't dine on hay or grains. Instead, they lived on the liquid swill, a by-product of beer and whiskey. At nearby breweries, barley, hops, corn, rye, and other grains were boiled into a mash and then distilled to make beer or grain alcohol.

Bergh breathed in the noxious stable odors as he listed graphic details in his notebook: "These foul prisons show man's stupidity and cruelty."

These breweries and distilleries sold the leftover wastes to dairies cheaply.

This poor-quality feed was all that cows ate, and drank. Cows produced swill milk that had a sickly bluish cast. Greedy dairy owners mixed in plaster of Paris, starch, eggs, and molasses to thicken the milk and make it a healthy hue. Despite the doctoring, not only was swill milk unhealthy, but it was hazardous to drink, and made children ill. This diseased milk often contained bovine tuberculosis, which could be passed to humans. And since the milk was watered down to make it stretch further, it was often contaminated by dirty water, hands, and containers that caused diseases such as cholera and typhoid.

Cows didn't fare any better: most milkers, the female cows who produced milk, died within six months of first being milked, never having left their manure-filled stalls. Their teeth rotted due to their alcoholic diet. Ulcers covered their udders. Only stumps remained where tails should be — a sign of diseased milkers.

Bergh breathed in the noxious stable odors as he listed graphic details in his notebook: "These foul prisons show man's stupidity and cruelty. Animals wallow in filth; some are tied by the neck in their narrow stalls by rope or chain; others are fastened by each horn so as to forbid movement; and in the trough before them is an acrid swill which no living creature would take into its stomach. In some instances, animals are actually dying while being milked."

Ironically, across New York this swill milk was sold as "Pure Orange County Milk."

Distillery dairy issues had been revealed several years before Bergh started the ASPCA. *Frank Leslie's Illustrated Newspaper* published an expose on swill dairies in 1858. That same year, the *New York Times* published an article, "How We Poison Our Children," declaring that swill milk "fatally poisoned 8,000 infants in this City."

Although dairies attempted to quiet the story, outrage from readers resulted in investigations. However, a politician with ties to distilleries headed the investigation. Michael Tuomey drank whiskey with the dairy owners and protected them. He intimidated witnesses who testified against the filthy stable conditions. Tuomey obstructed calls for reform and even argued that swill milk was healthy for children.

But Bergh had the tenacity of a terrier. He provoked the Board of Health to tour dairies in New York in 1870.

One reporter witnessed the slimy swill and wrote, "It took heroism on the part of Mr. Bergh and his companions to continue the inspection." Bergh prosecuted owners of the major swill dairies in an attempt to outlaw this vile fluid. Bergh lectured the Farmers' Club in 1878, describing how "by basely counterfeiting an indispensable article of food and imposing it on the unsuspecting for what it is not, health is destroyed, lingering and distressing diseases are induced, and life itself destroyed with impunity to say nothing of the torments inflicted on dumb animals."

Bergh's compassion for cows eventually led to an overhaul of the dairy business thanks to public outcry and new sanitary laws. Next, he tackled slaughterhouses, focusing his battle on the inhumane treatment of cattle and pursuing legislation to reduce suffering. "Now, is it not to be supposed that those who deal in the flesh and blood, the hides and hoofs, or animals brought from a great distance by rail, would use the best appliances to be had to prevent deterioration and death?" Bergh wrote. "Yet a visit to any cattle train proves the erroneousness of such an inference."

Bergh clashed with railways and shipping companies that transported livestock long distances, from America's western plains and feedlots to eastern slaughterhouses. The conditions on cattle trains jeopardized the meat supply.

AMERICAN PUBLIC HEALTH

As urban populations across America increased, so did human and industrial waste. Lemuel Shattuck, a teacher, conducted a sanitary survey in 1850. His *Report of the Sanitary Commission of Massachusetts* listed fifty visionary recommendations for public health practices. Shattuck pointed out that much of the ill health of city residents could be traced to unsanitary conditions. Mid-nineteenth-century New York had one of the highest mortality rates of U.S. cities. Cholera, typhus, yellow fever, and other diseases caused by poor sanitation contributed to this high rate. Dr. Stephen Smith waged a war to clean up the city and eradicate preventable diseases. The doctor directed a sanitary survey of the city in 1864. Smith's inspectors described stomach-churning findings: overflowing privies (outdoor toilets used by the entire neighborhood), cobblestone streets choked with garbage and manure from the 200,000 horses living in the city (each produced an average of twenty-two pounds daily), and slaughterhouses and rendering firms situated between crowded tenements. One inspection traced a stream of animal blood and liquid remains flowing from a Thirty-Ninth Street slaughterhouse to the river two blocks away. Smith's survey resulted in immediate sanitary improvements in New York. The state passed the first comprehensive health legislation in America in 1866.

One reform required cattle cars to contain water troughs, which prevented livestock from dying of thirst. Despite this improvement, animals endured horrendous conditions during their long journey. Some died of suffocation in unventilated boxcars, especially during warm weather. Most suffered from crippling injuries as they kicked and trampled each other in overcrowded cars. All starved, losing massive amounts of weight, since feed was withheld. Railroads anticipated losses — six percent of cattle and nine percent of sheep — under these adverse circumstances, but the shippers could always replenish the stock inexpensively with more from the plentiful western plains.

The powerful and wealthy railroad industry opposed any reforms. A delegation from the ASPCA was granted a hearing to state facts before the House Committee on Agriculture. However, the railroad lobby managed to shut down any investigation. Bergh lamented this ruthlessness: "[It] cannot be suppressed or even diminished, because of the despotic power of the tyrant of the age we live in — King Railroad!"

Livestock who survived the journey faced more brutal treatment as they were unloaded from the cars at terminals along the Hudson River. Handlers gouged cattle with sharp bladed sticks while rushing them to the slaughterhouse. Some animals destined for foreign dinner tables were then shipped from New York docks across the North Atlantic. These creatures received similar sadistic treatment, freezing on open decks and slipping and crushing each other during storms.

Survivors of the cattle cars were not dealt a swift and painless death when they finally entered one of the 250 slaughterhouses and meatpacking plants dotting the neighborhood south of West Fourteenth Street and from Hudson Street to the Hudson River. Here, livestock were treated like inanimate objects, without any acknowledg-

ment of the pain and terror they suffered before they were slaughtered. Bergh admonished those who made a living killing livestock, using flowery language to preach in slaughterhouses: "Remember, the same starlit night that brings you rest shines down also upon the blood-stained stones of your slaughterhouses and upon the dumb, despairing sufferers there."

Bergh was not a vegetarian. However, he insisted that animals in slaughterhouses be swiftly butchered. After trudging through the ankle-deep blood flowing through a Manhattan slaughterhouse while witnessing suffering, Bergh asked the butcher, "How can you sleep at night after such daily horror?"

The ASPCA president discovered a slaughterhouse where butchers heaved pigs into boiling water. "The laws of God and man are against this cruelty to helpless animals," he said. "I appeal to your manhood to help me in saving unnecessary suffering."

Butchers responded by flinging slaughterhouse offal at Bergh. But the ASPCA president never abused his power by arresting butchers for their malicious acts. Instead, he wiped off his face and stopped off at the chemist's shop, where stains could be removed from his overcoat.

Along with livestock, Bergh championed chickens. He alerted authorities to foul play during the slaughter of fowl. He charged a chicken butcher with cruel treatment, asserting that the animals were still alive when they were plucked and boiled.

In court, the defendant asked for the case to be dismissed. He informed the judge that he stabbed the chickens in their brains before plucking their feathers and plopping their bodies into boiling water. Bergh countered that it would be more humane to decapitate the chickens. However, since they were sold by weight, chickens containing their heads brought a higher price. The judge found in favor of the butcher, ruling that cruelty had not been proven.

Bergh targeted the inhumane yet routine practices of his day, demanding reform in dairies and slaughterhouses. He was determined to "put a stop to these hellish practices." Bergh's struggle for reforms was motivated by his conviction that all animals deserved kindness. In time, more people would share the ASPCA president's conviction that animals could suffer terror and felt pain — novel concepts in Bergh's era.

Chapter Nine
COMPASSION
FOR CANINES

The small terrier mix raced in circles, going nowhere. He ran inside a turnspit — a rotating treadmill resembling a large exercise wheel for pet rodents. The wheel was fixed to a chain that ran down to an iron spit.

The dog's paw power constantly turned this spit so that roasts would cook evenly over a fire pit. The turnspit dog had been bred for a distinctive shape: a long body with short, crooked front legs similar to those of today's basset hound. This allowed him to run for hours. He also had strong muscles in order to turn roasts and hams that weighed up to thirty pounds.

The naturalist Charles Darwin wrote, "Look at the

spit dog. That's an example of how people can breed animals to suit particular needs."

Charles Darwin: The Father of Evolution

Charles Darwin (1809–1882) was born in England on the same day that the future president Abraham Lincoln was born in Kentucky. As a boy, Darwin preferred chemistry to the classics, which earned him the nickname Gas. Later, at Edinburgh University, Darwin studied medicine. But a career as a doctor was not in his future: surgery nauseated him, and he detested anatomy.

At the university, Darwin mingled with freethinkers. These students had scientific views that were at odds with religious beliefs. They argued that animals had all the same mental powers as humans, such as the ability to reason.

After quitting medicine, Darwin transferred to Christ's College in Cambridge, where he trained for the ministry. However, a career as a priest did not appeal to Darwin either. Instead, his interest was spiked by botany, zoology, and geography.

When Darwin was twenty-two, he began a five-year journey circumnavigating the globe aboard the HMS *Beagle*.

On this scientific expedition he found fossils of extinct animals and studied specimens of plants and animals. The budding naturalist collected notes along with questions. He wondered, for example, how the thirteen species of finches on the Galápagos Islands were related yet "modified for different ends."

The key, Darwin concluded, was survival of the fittest. Each finch had adapted to the food supply in its environment by developing a different-size and different-shaped beak designed for long-term survival.

Darwin concentrated on his theory that all life on earth has evolved. He believed that plants and animals gradually developed from common ancestors. These species competed for food, water, and space in an unending struggle to survive and have more offspring.

He observed how this process of natural selection worked. Those plants and animals best suited to survival thrived, while those that failed to evolve disappeared. Then successful species passed on their advantageous characteristics to future generations. Over millions of years, natural selection could even change species, transforming dinosaurs into birds, and apes into humans.

Darwin wrote about his ideas in On the Origin of Species. His book was both controversial and groundbreaking when it was published in 1859. People raced to read it, and the first printing sold out in one day.

His theory of evolution alarmed religious Victorian society

with the idea that humans descended from earlier primates. It contradicted the creation story in the Book of Genesis, in which God created humans similar to their present form. Darwin was ridiculed by cartoonists who attached the head of the bearded naturalist onto the body of an ape.

Many scientists, however, agreed with Darwin's theory. They believed that evolution would continue onward to new heights. Darwin's fame as a naturalist spread around the world as his book was translated into various languages. His theory of evolution sparked international scientific debates that continue today.

The dog panted from the heat and exertion, but if he stopped he would be rewarded with a beating or, even worse, the cook would toss a hot coal into his wheel to motivate him to move faster. The turnspit terrier drooled as he sniffed the roasting meat, but not a morsel would be his.

Some turnspit dogs, such as this one, worked in tandem so that the spit constantly rotated its roasts. After hours of running, the exhausted dog was replaced with another, who would start his slavish shift in the restaurant kitchen. Their shared task supposedly led to the proverb "every dog has his day." These dogs were always on duty, including on the Sabbath, when they served as foot warmers during church services.

Bergh watched as the first dog collapsed on the dirt floor. Then he rapped his silver-headed walking stick on the window to attract the proprietor's attention.

These two turnspit terriers were about to be liberated.

Unfortunately, upon returning to the restaurant to make certain that the dogs were no longer being used to turn the spit, Bergh was shocked to discover that they had been replaced with African American children.

CHILD LABOR IN AMERICA

In Bergh's time, child labor, including indentured servitude and child slavery, was commonplace in United States cities. In 1870, the first year the census listed child laborers, about 750,000 workers age fifteen and under toiled in various industries, with an estimated 100,000 working in New York City. Most worked seventy or more hours per week under dangerous conditions, earning low pay that went to support their families. Factory owners hired children to run machines and haul loads because they were a source of cheap labor and less likely than adults to strike. City factories needed children to help churn out garments, glass items, paper boxes, envelopes, artificial flowers, buttons, paper collars, twine, and tobacco products. Other children worked in restaurants and blacksmith shops, ran errands, and sold newspapers. A national child labor law was not created until 1938, when Congress passed the Fair Labor Standards Act, which banned oppressive child labor and set federal standards and age restrictions.

Few dogs enjoyed status as pampered pets in the mid-nineteenth century. Most were doomed to endure lives of drudgery.

Dogs powered treadmills for other uses besides roasting spits, such as pumping water, churning butter, pressing fruit into cider, and grinding grains. There was even a patent issued for a sewing machine that could be powered by a turnspit dog.

These hard-working dogs were treated as pieces of machinery. Bergh described an unfortunate terrier struggling to power a treadmill attached to a cider press in a saloon. "The underside of [the dog's] collar had chafed a raw sore. . . . He panted and frequently tried to stop, but was so tied that he had to keep on running or choke." Bergh had the saloon owner arrested. The accused was convicted of cruelty, but appealed all the way to the state supreme court. Finally he received a hefty fine of twenty-five dollars.

Encouraged by this conviction, Bergh stormed into other New York City saloons that imprisoned turnspit dogs. He threatened arrest and, if challenged, brandished his walking stick. According to Bergh, the saloon owners "could not see how it was any of [his] business how they worked their cider mill. What was a dog for anyhow if he wasn't put to something? Was he only fit to be patted on his head?"

Other canines labored as beasts of burden. They pulled small carts for people who made a living scavenging rags and other refuse. Ragpickers used a tasty treat to lure stray dogs into service. After a backbreaking day of work, instead of being treated humanely, the unfortunate dogs were unharnessed to forage for food in the city's garbage cans and seek shelter in alleys.

Some canines had a career as coach dogs. They ran alongside carriages and wagons to keep the horses from spooking and to guard the contents. Their difficult job entailed running long distances while dodging perils such as horses' hooves and speeding vehicles.

Fighting dogs were valued as long as they came out on top. Although illegal in most states, these sadistic competitions attracted spectators who gambled on the outcome. Bergh denounced this cruel underground blood sport. "A sport should not be the enjoyment of cruelty and bloodshed. This shows our barbarism," he said. "Americans seek diversion and amusement but they are not willing to give over their country to bloody and demoralizing scenes." He believed that "the civilization of a people is indicated by their treatment of animals."

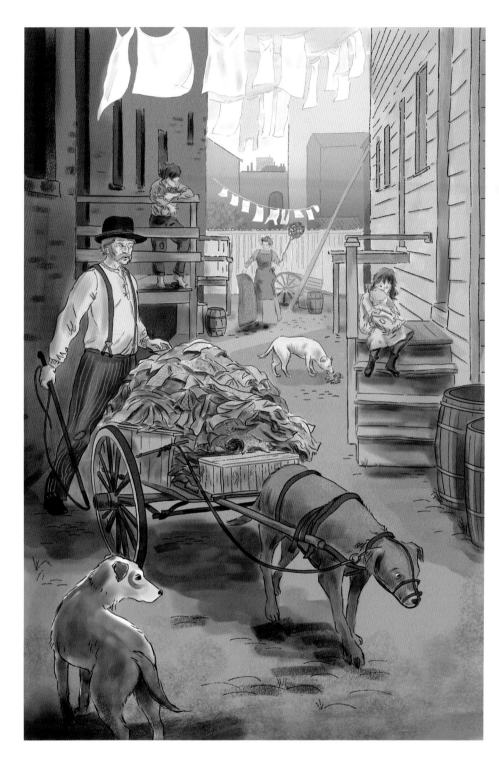

Ragpickers used a tasty treat to lure stray dogs into service.

The ASPCA president had been vigilantly planning a raid on Sportsmen's Hall prior to jumping through a skylight into the middle of a dogfighting pit that night in 1866. Christopher "Kit" Burns ran his profitable pit in the basement of Sportsmen's Hall, a tough tavern at 273 Water Street in Lower Manhattan. This notorious ringleader brashly advertised different types of dogfights several times a week.

One type was called a rat fight, in which a terrier was pitted against one hundred rats. Boys snatched brown rats from docks and garbage dumps and sold them to Burns for five cents apiece. At the start of the fight, the squirming rats scurried around a four-foot-deep zinc-lined pit for five minutes. There was no escape.

Then the dog handler tossed in a terrier. In seconds, rats had sunk their fangs into every inch of the dog, while the dog snapped at the rats. A *Tribune* reporter remarked, "The rapidity with which a well trained dog kills rats is astounding to the uninitiated . . . he bites to kill every time, and usually does it."

The battle raged for thirty to forty minutes as spectators drank, cheered, and betted on how long it would take the dog to slay the rats. It ended when every rat was killed. Sometimes the rats won the fight. Losers of both species were buried in the dirt beneath the pit's bleachers.

But the show wasn't over yet. Burns's son-in-law could be persuaded, for the cost of a beer, to bite a live rat in half.

Dogs also battled bears in the first-floor amphitheater. This barbaric blood sport resembled medieval bearbaiting, in which bulldogs ripped apart tethered black bears. Handlers set bulldogs upon a chained bear whose teeth and claws had been filed down. Gamblers bet on which of the beasts would survive. Top dogs chomped onto the bear's nose or throat, attempting to force the bruin to his knees, and didn't let go until handlers pried apart their jaws. The animal gladiators battled to the death.

Dogfighting in the 1860s resembled today's still-illegal "sport," in which humans encourage dogs to be brutal. However, humane treatment of animals was a new concept in that era. In 1867, Bergh revised New York's animal cruelty law to make all types of animal fighting illegal for the first time. The law forbade citizens to "maliciously kill, maim, wound, injure, torture or cruelly beat any animal belonging to himself or another." Violators faced a fine of one hundred dollars.

A newspaper article from 1868 condemned the illegal dogfighting at Sportsmen's Hall as "simply sickening." It asked readers to imagine the dogs "surrounded by a crowd of brutal wretches whose conduct stamps them as beneath the struggling beasts, and they will have a fair idea of the scene at Kit Burns's."

Burns's top fighting dogs lived on the second floor of Sportsmen's Hall, where they were trained in canine combat. He toughened his dogs by forcing them to run for hours on "the Wheel," a spinning turntable, as they attempted to battle growling and barking dogs who were chained nearby. The dogs ran around in circles for hours, their speed accelerating with their fury. These fighters practiced on expendable dogs who were kept warehoused in the basement's wooden stalls.

PIT BULLS: DEVOTED FRIENDS

The name "pit bull" includes a variety of related "bully" breeds and mixes, such as the American pit bull terrier, American Staffordshire terrier, and Staffordshire bull terrier. These compact, muscled dogs with wide mouths look tough, but are devoted friends when properly socialized and trained. They are known for their courage, loyalty, and strength.

Pit bulls descended from the Old English bulldog, a breed that originated in England between 1600 and 1700. Bulldogs were used to bait bulls, a blood "sport" in which dogs attacked a tethered bull and gamblers bet on the outcome. The British Parliament banned bullbaiting in 1835.

Unfortunately, people demanded a new blood sport. Breeders selectively bred bulldogs with terriers to create the pit bull prototype. This agile, athletic dog was a canine gladiator designed to fight other dogs. The fighters were rigorously trained so they would attack their four-legged opponents without flinching or hesitation. However, pit bulls were bred not to bite humans in order for handlers to manage their dogs during staged fights. Dogs who behaved aggressively toward humans were killed so that this undesirable trait was not passed on to future generations.

When immigrants sailed to America, their pit bulls were aboard the ships. Some were destined to continue the dogfighting tradition in cities. Others were valued for their work ethics. They herded cattle and sheep on the frontier. They protected livestock from bandits and wild animals. They helped catch hogs. And they guarded their families.

Pit bulls were also valued as companions. These protective dogs became known as the "nanny dog" because of their gentle and affectionate nature as a family dog. They took their responsibility for babysitting young children seriously. But they also enjoyed playing and had a great sense of humor!

Brave pit bulls would become America's military mascot during World War I (1914–19), starring on various patriotic posters. They would go on to excel as police dogs, search and rescue dogs, drug and bomb detection dogs, and therapy dogs. And they would continue to be popular family pets thanks to their good-natured personalities.

Yet pit bulls would also get a rotten reputation after unscrupulous people continued to breed them for illegal dogfighting (today a felony in all fifty states). Gangs and drug dealers used badly bred and poorly trained pit bulls as guard dogs. Negative publicity has resulted in breed-specific legislation (BSL) banning pit bulls in various communities.

Any breed of dog can become dangerous when raised to be aggressive. Many "bully" dogs are ambassadors for their breed. Recognizing this, twelve states have passed laws prohibiting BSL. Someday pit bulls' tarnished reputation could be restored and the dogs resume their rightful place as cherished companions.

Burns boldly advertised his dogfights by plastering posters around Water Street. Spectators jammed the hall, filling every seat in the stadium. Dogs ripped their opponents apart as handlers spurred them on. One spectator described how a losing pit bull's head was "a mass of blood, her jaws, jagged and torn, one ear torn away and not a kick left in her."

After Bergh and his ASPCA officer leapt into the dog-fighting pit, they arrested Burns, but the judge dismissed the case as Bergh hadn't caught Burns goading the dogs to fight. The animal fight promoter insisted that the interrupted fight was an "accident" because the dogs had escaped from their cages. Burns could not be found guilty of a crime unless caught in the act of urging the dogs to clash.

The proprietor of Sportsmen's Hall badgered Bergh. "Your society is doing a noble work, sir, yes, a magnificent work, but let me tell you, when it interferes in dog fighting, it digs its own grave."

Several years later, in November of 1870, Bergh finally quashed Burns by getting the evidence needed to close down the blood-spattered walls of Sportsmen's Hall. Burns never went to jail, dying before his case was tried. His hall experienced a turnabout, hosting religious revival meetings.

In 1875, Bergh introduced a dog- and cockfighting bill that passed. The law allowed him to arrest the fight organizers as well as spectators, and gave him the power to seize the animals. If fight organizers fled to different cities, Bergh alerted other independent SPCAs in those regions. These societies would attempt to rehabilitate the former fighting dogs and adopt them into kind homes.

When fighting dogs became injured and working dogs too old to toil, they were easily replenished. Packs of stray dogs crowded city streets, and were considered a public health threat because of the diseases they often carried. The majority suffered dreadful fates.

A century before Bergh patrolled the streets, George Washington observed, "The canine species in New York is friendless." The president had been commenting on a rabies panic, which put wandering dogs in danger of being killed.

One hundred years later, people still erroneously believed that sweltering weather caused dogs to go mad with rabies. New York City devised a summer special: fifty cents for each stray dog rounded up and delivered to the pound. The dogs' families had until late afternoon to pay a two-dollar fee to liberate their pets.

Strays housed in the city-run shelter in Brooklyn were not treated compassionately. They were crammed into a shed with no food or water. An article that appeared in the *World* described how the pound operated "in a manner greatly detrimental to the public health and the dogs [were] treated in a most inhumane manner."

The city replaced civilians with official dogcatchers, but stray canines fared no better. A bounty was paid per dog, so many catchers stole dogs straight from people's yards. Then they extorted a redemption fee, threatening to drown the dog unless it was paid. The thieving catchers knew they would not be punished, as courts maintained that dogs were not property.

The stray dog situation demanded reform. For Bergh, this injustice must have reminded him of a childhood battle he fought with neighborhood bullies who attempted to drown stray dogs and cats in the East River.

Yet some criticized Bergh for not meddling when the dogs in the city pound were executed by drowning. The ASPCA president responded with a wishy-washy justification. "It does not necessarily follow that there is cruelty in taking animal life; otherwise the butcher exposes himself to this charge, and all who eat flesh are to a certain extent, accomplices," he responded. "In the case of the dogs, it is more a question of death than cruelty, and I am free to confess that I am not quite satisfied in my own mind whether life or speedy dissolution is most to be coveted by man or beast in this hot and disagreeable world."

Bergh did battle New York City's effort to round up and kill dogs based on the groundless fear of rabies.

He wrote the mayor, detailing the fallacies behind the rabies scare. Bergh could not find any cases of humans catching rabies from the bite of a stray dog. He ended his letter imploring "that the wholesale slaughter of these faithful companions of our race [could] be dispensed with without detriment to ... moral, physical and pecuniary interests."

Next, his ASPCA strived to get all dogs licensed. The license fees were used to operate several shelters where lost, stray, and injured dogs could find sanctuary. (Their feline counterparts had not yet been elevated to pet status; cats were free to stray the streets. They were, however, covered by the law, as the ASPCA's first annual report confirmed in 1867 when it reported that a criminal had been sentenced to ten days in jail for beating a cat to death. A twenty-five-dollar fine was tacked on to his punishment after he stated that "the arresting officer ought to be disemboweled.")

Bergh made certain that strays were treated with compassion. In the new, modern shelter built in New York City, dogs were housed in clean, well-ventilated stalls stuffed with hay, and had access to food, water, and a spot to exercise. Unclaimed dogs were euthanized humanely with gas.

The "Canine Bath Tub"

Stray dogs roamed the city streets, where most met a tragic end, either starving or succumbing to injuries. Since females were not spayed and males were not neutered, the tragedy continued as litters of unwanted puppies accelerated the overpopulation crisis.

Dogcatchers seized stray dogs and impounded them for twenty-four hours. Few people claimed or adopted these dogs. Their fate was not euthanasia, which translates from the Greek as "an easy or happy death." Instead, unwanted dogs were drowned. One part of the river at the end of East Twenty-Sixth Street was euphemistically known as the "canine bath tub."

A newspaper article described how 762 out of 782 dogs were drowned during one day in July 1877. "A large crate, seven feet long, four high and five broad, made of iron bars set three inches apart, was rolled up the aisles, and the dogs, about 48 at a time, were dropped into it through a sliding top door. The crate was then wheeled out to the water's edge, where it was attached to a crane, elevated, swung out and dropped into the river, where it was kept submerged 10 minutes, then it was lifted up, emptied and returned for another load. The carcasses were disposed of to the rendering establishment at the foot of twenty-eighth-street, where it is said, their hides have an average value of $1 apiece."

The article noted that the "dogs seemed to know their fate, and most of them sullenly submitted to it; but many crouched down desperately in their corners, and made a most ferocious and dangerous resistance." While the drownings were taking place, dogcatchers had rounded up 675 more stray dogs who would meet the same fate the next day.

Euthanasia in America

Bergh sought more humane methods to rid the streets of unwanted dogs. When the ASPCA president discovered that the city of Buffalo was using electricity to euthanize strays, he wrote to America's top inventor, Thomas Alva Edison. The inventor requested that Bergh provide "some good-sized animals" so Edison could run his own experiments to determine the minimum voltage required to kill a dog. Bergh adamantly refused, reiterating that the ASPCA's aim was "instantaneous and merciful death" for strays. "To me there is always something indescribably sad in the word 'kill,'" Bergh said.

Other methods of killing strays, which later included cats, were also unacceptable, as they did not result in an instant painless death. They included shooting the animals, administering drugs such as strychnine, injecting lethal drugs into the heart, putting animals in gas chambers and asphyxiating them with a gas such as carbon monoxide, and putting them in sealed high-altitude decompression chambers in which they suffocated when air was rapidly removed. A peaceful and kind death could only be achieved by an intravenous lethal injection of sodium pentobarbital, which remains the modern method of humanely euthanizing abandoned animals.

Today, approximately 75 percent of dogs in the United States are altered (spayed or neutered), and adoptions from animal shelters are robust — both of which have dramatically reduced the numbers of animals euthanized, although the number hovers in the heart-wrenching figure of four million per year. According to the latest available statistics in 2013, New York City has the lowest euthanasia rate of cats and dogs per capita for any major U.S. city. Animal advocates believe that, in the near future, New York shelters will adopt a no-kill policy, where all healthy animals will be adopted into loving homes.

Despite the urging of New York officials, Bergh refused to run the city pound. Animal welfare, not animal control, was the ASPCA's focus. "This Society could not stultify its principles so far as to encourage the tortures which the proposed give rise to," Bergh wrote. His society would not accept New York City's money to kill unwanted dogs. Its mission was to reduce animal suffering and save lives, not end them.

Chapter Ten
"CIVILIZED" BLOOD SPORTS

On January 5, 1872, sportsmen lined up with their shotguns at the entrance of Fleetwood Park. Competitors paid their twenty-five-dollar entrance fee in the hopes of winning a prize at the grand pigeon-shooting tournament. James Gordon Bennett, prosperous publisher of the *New York Herald,* would present a silver cup as the first prize. The second prize would be cash.

Pigeon shooting was considered a gentlemen's pastime. As they waited for the traps to be released, the high-society sportsmen discussed their strategies for targeting and hitting the live birds.

The marksmen debated the top methods used to ensure that the pigeons flew in lively flight patterns, making them more challenging targets. Some birds had pins jabbed under their wings. Others had caustic substances such as pepper or turpentine smeared in one eye to blind them.

One man recalled a pigeon shoot eight years earlier in England when an assistant twisted off pigeons' legs before he released the birds from the trap. The crippled pigeons flew slower and were an easier target, giving one shooter a competitive edge over another. The RSPCA lodged a cruelty complaint against the assistant.

The men reminisced as they watched a pigeon box being set up in the ring for the opening of the match. In a few moments, the first of a thousand birds would be released and the first shooter would have two attempts to shoot the pigeon dead inside the ring.

No shots were ever fired. T. W. Hartfield, the general superintendent of the ASPCA, waved a warrant that would break up the match. He commanded a squad of brave officers who bodily blocked the traps from the marksmen to prevent shooting.

Bergh adamantly opposed all animal cruelty, whether it was lowbrow dogfighting attracting audiences mainly composed of the lower echelon, or fashionable

In a few moments, the first of a thousand birds would be released and the first shooter would have two attempts to shoot the pigeon dead inside the ring.

pigeon shoots favored by moneyed sportsmen.

Although some of these sportsmen had donated generously to his society, the ASPCA president took the risk of angering other potential donors with deep pockets when he attacked sports favored by the gentry. He detested any "sports" in which people tortured and killed innocent creatures for entertainment.

He opposed fox hunting, in which hunters on horseback trailed a pack of scent hounds who would track, chase, and tear apart a red fox. He despised hare coursing, in which two sight hounds competed in a deadly race to chase, catch, and kill a hare. He abhorred the hounding of the deer, another blood sport, in which dogs drove the deer into water so hunters could slaughter them.

"Dog hunting and water butchery are not sport," Bergh stated. "It is simply murder."

He wrote farmers who lived on Long Island, requesting that they help him quash the attempt to introduce fox hunting in their neighborhood. The farmers reacted with indifference. Bergh predicted that thieves and tramps soon would occupy Long Island. "Figs do not grow on thistles," he said, "and if the devil be at the head of a people it is simply because the people are devilish."

And he spoke out against pigeon shoots. In these competitions, thousands of birds were shot for fun. As shotguns blasted, the pigeons tumbled to the ground in pain, with broken backs and wings. Some birds died instantly, while the injured faced a worse fate: suffering before succumbing to their wounds.

Sportsmen insisted that the pigeon target practice was patriotic. It would prepare them to defend their country during wartime.

Bergh wasn't buying this twisted logic. "Then why not man hunting instead," he snapped. "This would be better preparation!"

In a letter to the *New York Times*, Bergh lambasted pigeon shooting as a "cruel and unmanly 'sport.'"

He expressed disgust that people were "capable of deriving pleasure from the mutilation and agony of one of the tamest and most gentle of all the feathered race."

Determined to save pigeons from this gruesome fate, Bergh introduced a bill that would ban these shoots. Lawmakers amended the bill, releasing the shooters from accountability for cruelty if maimed pigeons were humanely destroyed.

Bergh also helped develop and promote trapshooting as a humane alternative. The gyropigeon, a steel bird with extended wings, could be projected from a spring trap to simulate a pigeon in flight. The clay pigeon, a target shaped like a saucer, could be propelled into the air from traps at high speeds. These inventions substituted artificial for live, saving birds from the sportsman's gun.

The ASPCA president was also on the scene when a Spanish matador attempted to host a bullfighting event in New York City. More than three decades had passed since Bergh had attended his first bullfight in Spain. Now, in 1880, he had the power to prevent the type of bloodshed that had changed the course of his life.

The matador promised that the fight would be bloodless, with bulls being stuck with gummed ribbon rosettes on their foreheads instead of being stabbed with lances.

Bergh and a dozen of his officers attended the spectacle, along with three thousand paying spectators. "There seems to be an appetite among men for anything that savors of cruelty," Bergh told a *New York Herald* reporter. "If this sport should become popular here we would soon be reduced to the level of Spanish character, and nothing would satisfy the public but blood."

The gentry arrived at the makeshift arena on 116th Street in horse-drawn carriages and attended by liveried servants. However, the promised combat quickly degenerated into more bull than fight. The eight Spanish matadors jumped over the fence each time a Texas steer (masquerading as a bull) came close. Only one matador succeeded in sticking rosettes on a bull's forehead.

Bergh need not have worried about New York hosting future bullfights. The next morning he could read the *New York Herald*'s editorial stating, "Driving a frightened steer into a ring and then daubing him all over with bunches of ribbons fastened to adhesive plasters is not an exhilarating sight, even when the two-legged performers prance about in tinsel dresses."

Chapter Eleven

BATTLING BARNUM

Superintendent Hartfield of the ASPCA stormed into the circus ring trailed by seven of his agents and a squad of twenty police officers. The entourage was not there to enjoy "The Greatest Show on Earth." Instead, they were there at Bergh's command to stop the circus's main attraction.

Phineas Taylor (P. T.) Barnum had broadcast that Salamander the Fire Horse would be jumping through flaming hoops on the afternoon of April 20, 1880. Barnum's circus was the largest in America, covering five acres and attracting crowds of 10,000 paying patrons. Posters advertised Salamander's "daring & dangerous equestrian act."

Bergh demanded that Barnum discontinue the performance. He condemned the feat as "an act of cruelty and terror," and wrote Barnum that it was "simply abominable that the public cannot be provided with amusement by your show without inflicting torture upon an animal."

The showman attempted to clarify that the "fire" rings blazed with artificial flames, produced by harmless chemicals that emitted no heat. The Great Meddler, however, refused to listen. He sent Hartfield to stop Salamander from performing.

Barnum was ready. He gave a speech to the audience awaiting the show. "I shall place a hoop of fire around Henry Bergh that will make him warmer than he has been in the past and probably than he will ever experience in the future!" he promised.

Then the showman announced he would star in the act. According to the local newspaper, Barnum "vaulted about with admirable agility," leaping through the fire hoops. A dozen clowns, Salamander, and even Superintendent Hartfield followed Barnum. Not one hair was singed.

The Great Showman triumphed over the Great Meddler, and not for the first time.

P. T. Barnum had broadcast that Salamander the Fire Horse would be jumping through flaming hoops.

The animal activist and the "patron saint of promoters," as *Life* magazine dubbed Barnum, had locked horns in 1866, the same year that the ASPCA formed.

Barnum's American Museum was a smash hit — the Disney World of the nineteenth century. Inside the museum, located on Broadway, spectators gawked at human exhibits, such as the performing midget "General" Tom Thumb, who stood twenty-five inches tall, and exotic animals, including a den of lions, a Bengal tiger, and a grizzly bear.

Barnum advertised his museum as the home of "millions of curiosities." To entice spectators into paying the twenty-five-cent entry fee, Barnum displayed boa constrictors in the public exhibition room as a source of entertainment. His zookeeper periodically stocked the cage with live doves and rabbits. The snake would squeeze its prey to kill it and then swallow it whole. After such a meal, the boa constrictor would not feed again for weeks.

Outraged, Bergh visited the museum to complain about an "amusement which consists in the prolonged torture of an innocent creature." When the manager did not have this "evil corrected," Bergh wasted no time "protesting against the cruel mode of feeding the snake which is there on exhibition." The ASPCA president dashed off a letter to Barnum stating, "Any person who can commit an atrocity such as the one I complain of . . . is semi-barbarian in his instincts."

Thanks to Bergh's strong influence, Barnum was forced to board his snakes in the Taylor Hotel in Jersey City, New Jersey, where they dined without an audience. Now it was the showman's turn to be outraged. "Your arbitrary conduct . . . compelled my associates to send their reptiles to a neighboring state to be fed," Barnum wrote Bergh. The ASPCA's legal arm did not extend across the Hudson River to New Jersey.

But once again, Barnum found a way to gain free publicity at Bergh's expense. He contacted Professor Agassiz, the Harvard zoologist, who declared (incorrectly) that boa constrictors would die unless given food that was alive.

"I do not think the most active member of the society would object to eating lobster salad because the lobster was boiled alive, or refuse roasted oysters because they were cooked alive, or raw oysters because they must be swallowed alive," Agassiz added.

In a letter, Bergh challenged Agassiz, the very expert he had relied upon during the turtle trials: "It may be urged that these reptiles will not eat dead food — in reply to this I have to say, then let them starve. . . . But, I am satisfied that this assertion is false in theory and practice, for no living creature will allow itself to perish of hunger, with food before it, be the ailment dead or alive."

The letters flew back and forth, fast and furious, in this public battle between the activist and the promoter. Barnum, always the showman, sent his collection of snake incident correspondence with Bergh to the *Evening Post*. Barnum chastised Bergh's behavior, saying that it revealed "low breeding and a surplus of self-conceit."

Another newspaper, the *New York World*, later published the entire collection of letters between the two adversaries. It poked fun at Bergh, commenting, "The snake controversy is funny as well as instructive." While the ASPCA president's dignity was damaged, he did not cease provoking the showman.

Bergh blamed Barnum for "incarcerating poor helpless dumb beasts in iron cages within the tinder-like walls" when the original American Museum burned to the ground in 1865. The fire drew a crowd of 30,000 gawkers. Its cause was never discovered. Visitors and performers managed to escape. So did some animals: birds soared into the sky after an employee opened their cages, snakes slithered to freedom, and a seal was rescued by a firefighter. Other creatures were not so fortunate. Lions, monkeys, polar bears, and zebras perished in their cages; a pair of beluga whales boiled in their tank.

A mere six weeks after the devastating fire, Barnum opened the doors to his new American Museum, which had been rebuilt several blocks to the north. One of the ASPCA's supporters found the animal exhibits at the new museum unacceptable. He dashed off a letter to Bergh: "Speaking, Sir, of inhumanity to the brute creation — I would ask, is not Barnum's whole establishment one of cruelty to the Animal Creation?"

The letter writer added that in Europe, animal exhibitions were located in open gardens. "Barnum's affair is nothing more than a few stores knocked into one and with an atmosphere not only calculated to inflict the beasts with sickness but alike dangerous to visitors. In case of fire, so common in New York, what escape for the poor beasts; none whatever."

Three years later fire again destroyed Barnum's American Museum. This time, all the animals struggled in vain to escape from their locked cages. Firefighters attempted to battle the blazes, but frigid temperatures turned the water from their hoses into ice. Barnum lamented the fate of the "poor animals," and he had no interest in reviving the museum from the ashes for the third time. Instead, the showman focused on the circus trade, forming "The Greatest Show on Earth."

The circus, too, provoked Bergh. In 1879, his ASPCA arrested one of Barnum's elephant trainers, who rammed a hot poker up a creature's trunk. The "burning method" was used to teach the elephant how to perform tricks.

Yet Bergh did not acknowledge the suffering of elephants when several circus-goers protested the use of bull hooks. Trainers forced elephants to perform by repeatedly using this weapon, a sharp hook at the end of a rod, to dig into sensitive skin behind the ears, on the trunk, and on the head. Bergh believed Barnum's misinformation that elephants have thick hides and therefore do not experience pain when struck with a bull hook. Conversely, Bergh should have realized that the reason bull hooks were such an effective means of training was that they inflicted pain.

THE HISTORY OF THE CIRCUS

Phineas Taylor Barnum (1810–1891) couldn't brag that he invented the first circus. However, the showman did shape the American circus experience: three rings beneath a big top where animals, acrobats, aerialists, and other acts performed.

His spectacular circus had its roots in ancient entertainment. Thousands of years ago, acrobats and jugglers performed in China and Egypt. Ancient Greeks danced on tightropes. Ancient Romans hosted the Circus Maximus, with chariot races and battles between gladiators and elephants. And during the Middle Ages, animal and human performers entertained audiences at fairs around Europe.

In 1768, a more modern circus debuted in England. There, Philip Astley showed off horse-riding tricks he learned in the military. The circular ring helped him keep his balance while standing upon the horse's back. Astley added a clown, musicians, jugglers, acrobats, tightrope walkers, and performing dogs to entertain audiences between riding tricks.

Rival trick riders and entertainers spread across Europe and soon landed in America. In 1793, the Scottish rider John Bill Ricketts brought his one-ring circus to Philadelphia. As his horse galloped around the ring, Ricketts leapt over a ribbon suspended twelve feet in the air and landed back in the saddle. Included in the audiences his troupe entertained was President

George Washington, who returned the following evening for a repeat performance. Ricketts added tricks and performers and took his show on the road.

Decades later, P. T. Barnum's Grand Traveling Museum, Menagerie, Caravan & Circus performed for the first time. The year was 1870, the circus was the largest in American history, and Barnum was sixty years old. His circus grossed $400,000 that first year (more than $7 million today).

By 1872, Barnum was billing his circus as "The Greatest Show on Earth." It spread across five acres and attracted crowds of 10,000 patrons at a time. But Barnum dreamed of gigantic audiences. He loaded his circus onto sixty-five railroad cars and crisscrossed America. Then he added a second ring in 1873, followed by a third in 1881. That year, Barnum teamed up with his competitor, James A. Bailey.

Barnum & Bailey's Greatest Show on Earth introduced a new word into the English language in 1882: *jumbo*. Barnum brought a colossal twelve-foot African elephant named Jumbo to America. "It is a fact that he is simply beyond comparison. The largest elephants I ever saw are mere dwarfs by the side of Jumbo," the showman said.

The show went on after Barnum died in 1891. His circus merged with the Ringling Bros. Circus in 1907. Today, their three-ring circus continues to tour across America. At the same time, many modern circuses, such as Cirque du Soleil, are moving in an innovative direction: they travel the world with the spotlight on human, not animal, performers. The Ringling Bros. and Barnum & Bailey Circus has plans in place to end the use of elephants in their shows by 2018.

Despite their acrimonious relationship, the two rivals eventually developed an unlikely friendship after Bergh succeeded in winning over Barnum, who became a grudging admirer.

The showman acknowledged that Bergh should be "honored and respected for his unselfish devotion to such an excellent cause." Barnum donated to the ASPCA, and started the Bridgeport Society for the Prevention of Cruelty to Animals in Connecticut. He even referred to himself as "the Bergh of Bridgeport."

Bergh also reversed his opinion of Barnum after the showman started contributing to anti-cruelty societies. Bergh called Barnum "one of the most humane and kind-hearted men living. He manages an exhibition which, in view of its vast magnitude and amazing excellence of details, has no equal in the world."

Bergh's gushing homage to Barnum neglected to criticize cruel circus practices, many of which continue today. The mistreatment of wild animals during training to teach them to perform unnatural tricks took place under the secrecy of the big top. Surely Bergh observed more than elephants being goaded with bull hooks. Did Barnum "vanquish" Bergh, as he bragged in his auto-biography, *Struggles and Triumphs*, quashing the ASPCA president's criticisms through hush money as his circus rose in popularity? Did Bergh, the model humanitarian and champion of animals, turn a blind eye to the cruel treatment of elephants and other circus animals? The answers are obscured in history.

When Barnum died in 1891, he willed a generous amount of money to the ASPCA along with a thousand dollars to the city of Bridgeport for a statue honoring Bergh. The monument of a horse was erected in October 1897 in Seaside Park, where it stands today. The ASPCA's medallion shield, portraying an avenging angel rising up to protect a flogged carriage horse, decorates two sides of the statue.

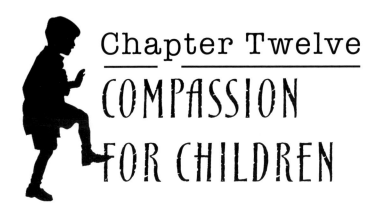

Chapter Twelve
COMPASSION
FOR CHILDREN

An officer carried a tiny sobbing child into the Manhattan courthouse on an April day in 1874. In one hand she clutched an enormous stick of peppermint candy — her sole possession.

Mary Ellen wore a filthy tattered dress beneath the horse blanket that had been wrapped around her. Black and blue marks inflicted by a rawhide whip covered her scarred body. A gash zigzagged through her left eyebrow and down her cheek. Although Mary Ellen was the size of a typical five-year-old child, in actuality the emaciated girl was nine.

A chilling silence accompanied Mary Ellen's testimony. She told Judge Lawrence of the Supreme Court, Bergh, and others that both of her parents were dead.

Mary Ellen explained that her guardian never let her outside of the rear tenement they shared in New York City's Hell's Kitchen. She described her bed as "only a piece of carpet stretched on the floor underneath a window" and how she lacked shoes and stockings in winter.

Mary Ellen testified that her guardian whipped her nearly every day and described how the woman used shears to carve the girl's face, narrowly missing her eye.

"I have no recollection of ever having been kissed by any one — have never been kissed by momma," Mary Ellen told the court. "I have never been taken on momma's lap or caressed or petted; I never dared speak to anybody, because if I did I would get whipped."

She confessed that she didn't know why she was whipped because her guardian never said anything during the beatings. "I do not want to go back to live with momma, because she beats me so," Mary Ellen said.

When the child concluded her heart-wrenching tale, a witness described how the stern-looking men in her audience wept aloud.

In 1874, when Mary Ellen's testimony took place, no anti-cruelty laws protected children. Parents abandoned infants on doorsteps. Abusive parents beat, burned, clubbed, and whipped their children. Some children traded the abuse for a life on the streets, begging for pennies.

Child labor laws regulating the minimum ages of employment and maximum hours of work would not be achieved until the 1938 Fair Labor Standards Act. Prior to that, American children slaved sixteen-hour workdays in factories, mines, and canneries. Owners chose children because they worked for lower wages, were easier to supervise, and were less likely to go on strike than adults.

Children eventually replaced the turnspit dogs, walking on treadmills in kitchens. Others worked on farms, in

home workshops, and as servants. The least lucky labored for criminals — stealing, picking pockets, and prostituting.

The mistreatment and exploitation of children was tackled in New York newspapers in the 1860s, but neither law enforcement nor charities got involved.

"The children of New York are sadly in need of a champion," observed the *New York Evening Telegram* in 1866. "It is not alone the lower animals that are subject to ill-treatment and cruelty," stated the *Northern Budget of Troy* in 1867.

Perhaps Etta Wheeler, a social worker for a charitable assistance organization, read these newspaper articles before the plight of Mary Ellen was brought to her attention in 1873 by a homebound woman who lived in the same tenement and heard Mary Ellen's cries. Wheeler visited the child's guardian, Mary Connolly, to assess the situation and was shocked by Mary Ellen's condition and became determined to rescue her.

When help from the police or from religious and charitable organizations wasn't forthcoming, Wheeler rationalized that the child was similar to an abused animal, and hurried to the ASPCA. She asked Bergh, "Is there anything more helpless than a defenseless child? If you can't interfere on other grounds, possibly you may find

Mary Ellen testified that her guardian whipped her nearly every day and described how the woman used shears to carve the girl's face, narrowly missing her eye.

some way of reaching this child on the grounds that it is an unfortunate little animal of the human race."

Bergh agreed to help. He believed that there was a link between the abuse of children and animals. "Men will be just toward men when they are charitable toward animals," he noted.

Besides, Bergh's critics always scolded him for being a misanthrope who helped animals instead of humans. One magazine editor passed judgment on Bergh in an article: "He wanders the landscape looking for abuses levied against dogs and cats, cows and cab horses. In his zeal he will stop a crowded omnibus if he feels that the horse drawing it is overworked. What ill-advised virtue is this when myriad children are being beaten and starved?" he wrote. "The young and weak of our own humanity are forced into heavy labor and suffering. Better that Mr. Bergh should tend to our own first, than waste his efforts on four footed beasts created by God to serve man's needs and pleasures."

Now Bergh could silence his critics and put his meddling to good use. "The child is an animal," he reasoned. "If there is no justice for it as a human being, it shall at least have the rights of the dog in the street. It shall not be abused."

Within forty-eight hours after Bergh first heard about the situation, "Little Mary Ellen," as she became known in the press, was rescued. She eventually was raised by Wheeler's sister and her husband, and later married, had two daughters, and lived to the age of ninety-two. Mary Ellen's persecutor was sentenced to one year in the penitentiary.

The case inspired Bergh to champion children's rights. He launched the New York Society for the Prevention of Cruelty to Children, the world's first child protection agency, on December 15, 1874.

"I regard a helpless child in the same light as a dumb animal," Bergh explained. "Both are God's creatures. Neither can protect themselves. My duty is imperative to aid them."

However, he cautiously kept the two societies separate, not wanting to dilute attention or support for either cause. Bergh served on the board, but appointed ASPCA lawyer Elbridge T. Gerry as president of the Society for the Prevention of Cruelty to Children. Bergh's priority continued to be animals.

Chapter Thirteen
THE GREAT MEDDLER

Despite the growing social movement against animal cruelty, Bergh collected critics who castigated him in public. This wealthy do-gooder made them suspicious. Some dubbed him an animal fanatic. Several politicians had been reluctant to support his petition for the ASPCA. They didn't want to extend legal rights to nonhumans.

Others mocked his concern for creatures. The famous artist Thomas Nast was one. Known as the "Father of the American Cartoon," Nast drew many political cartoons. He used his barbed wit to draw Bergh advising animals shivering in the winter to wear coats and hats. Nast also linked Bergh's concern for animals to Darwin's theory of evolution by drawing a gorilla asking for Bergh's protection.

THE POWER O

Political cartoonists have been stirring up controversy in America since 1754. That's when Benjamin Franklin's "Join, Or Die" cartoon was published. The image of a severed snake urged the thirteen colonies to band together as a single political unit.

America's first political cartoon appeared in the May 9, 1754, edition of the *Pennsylvania Gazette,* a newspaper owned and run by Franklin. Other drawings depicting political issues soon followed. They were posted on walls, printed in newspapers and magazines, and passed around in pamphlets.

Political cartoons express a strong viewpoint. They convey their message using visual details such as caricature, in which the subject's most prominent features are emphasized and exaggerated. These cartoons can be equal parts critical and humorous. By appealing to emotions, political cartoons aim to persuade viewers to accept opinions about current events and people in power.

Thomas Nast (1840–1902) was considered the father of American political cartooning. Although this German immigrant could not read or write, he would become one of the most influential cartoonists in history. Nast illustrated the political symbol of the elephant for the Republican Party and the popular image of Santa Claus as a jolly, rotund man in a red suit. When Nast became the featured cartoonist at *Harper's Weekly,* the leading illustrated newspaper of the nineteenth century, he focused on New York City politics. His caricatures

POLITICAL CARTOONS

of William Magear
"Boss" Tweed, published in
the magazine beginning in 1871,
helped bring down the most corrupt
politician in America.

Tweed, who defrauded the citizens of New York out of
two hundred million dollars, feared the power of Nast's
cartoons. These included "The Brains," which depicted Tweed's
head replaced by a moneybag to symbolize the money he
had stolen from New York City, and "Who Stole the People's
Money?," which showed Tweed and his gang standing in a circle,
each passing the blame by pointing his finger at his neighbor.

Nast became the scourge of Tweed and was determined to
topple the corrupt politician. Tweed attempted to halt the
cartoons. "Stop them damn pictures," he told his henchmen. "I
don't care a straw for your newspaper articles. My constituents
can't read. But they can't help seeing them damn pictures!"

When Nast continued exposing corruption through his
political cartoons, Boss Tweed attempted to bribe the cartoonist
with $500,000, ostensibly for a trip to Europe to study art. Nast
turned down the bribe, even though it was a hundred times his
annual salary. Tweed was sentenced to prison, but escaped to
Spain. There, a Spanish customs official recognized Tweed from
Nast's cartoons and apprehended the corrupt politician.

In a strange twist, Tweed's final resting place was
Green-Wood Cemetery, the same burial ground where Bergh
would be buried a decade later.

Other cartoons showed Bergh weeping at bull-fights and behind a loaded cart of stray dogs. One cartoon with the caption "It even makes the animals laugh" depicted Bergh with giant donkey ears (similar to those that "Humanity Dick" Martin wore in a political cartoon) surrounded by giggling creatures. Another, entitled "The Friend of the Brutes," showed him with two bulldogs dressed as ASPCA agents.

City newspapers took up the call to torment the ASPCA's president. The *New York Sunday Mercury*, which catered to an audience of sportsmen, ran with the donkey image. Its editorial labeled Bergh as "an ass that should have his ears cropped."

Another newspaper mocked, "Cockroaches ... insist on sharing the best. Rats insist on having a chair at the table ... goats put on airs ... hogs grunt with delight ... as unlimited sway is given to the very humane Bergh."

An article in *McClure's Magazine* described some people's "furious opposition to the Bergh Crusade." It noted that "the better classes were as bitterly intolerant as were the vindictive and cruel lower classes. Jeers, maledictions, threats of personal violence, or appeals to law, insults both veiled and open, he bore calmly." The article

Other cartoons showed Bergh weeping behind a loaded cart of stray dogs.

detailed how "a snapping, snarling crowd of lesser publications pursued him with ribald jest and coarse lampoon, while at theatres he was often alluded to in the most farcical and grotesque way."

Nothing could stop Bergh, not even a smattering of anonymous letters bearing threats against his life. Letters decorated with skulls and crossbones warned him to leave town, and one even forecast the exact date and time when he would be assassinated.

Some foes attempted to carry out their threats. A man who had been arrested for overloading his horse cart swung at Bergh with a piece of iron, missing him. Through it all, Bergh persevered in his struggle for animal protection.

"I fear neither disease nor ridicule," he wrote. "From early morning until ten o'clock at night, I am at work. My own private affairs are neglected and I am often scolded by Mrs. Bergh for not giving a little time to personal matters."

Bergh's wife was very supportive, offering encouragement when her husband's spirits sagged. She noted that often he would return home weighed down with sadness and frustration. Bergh would retreat upstairs to his room and have a "jolly good cry."

The next morning he would muster the courage to continue. "Two or three years of ridicule and abuse have thickened the epidermis of my sensibilities, and I have acquired the habit of doing the thing I think right, regardless of public clamor," he said. The ASPCA would not be tucking its tail between its legs — it was here to stay.

Although he had failed as a poet and playwright, Bergh discovered that he could write with authority about his passion. He composed magazine articles to explain how the ASPCA was taking action through arrests and court cases. He penned letters to the editors of the dozen daily newspapers flourishing in New York City. He used the power of his pen to persuade politicians to consider adopting his humane viewpoint. He wrote precise letters to judges and police captains giving exact details. "I have adopted a habit through life of always pursuing a subject until it is brought to its legitimate conclusion," he wrote to a justice.

The prolific writer also composed speeches and delivered them with eloquence. He spoke out against animal cruelty before church groups and schoolchildren. And his lecturing tour that wound through major cities in the American West resulted in the formation of several humane societies in that region.

He never passed up an opportunity to urge Americans to be humane to all creatures. When crowds gathered to watch the ASPCA president stop someone for a wrongdoing, Bergh would discuss kindness. This frequent speech became known as his curbstone address.

The president of the ASPCA believed that "to plant, or revive, the principle of mercy in the human heart" would be "a triumph . . . greater than the building of the Great Pacific Railroad." Gradually, as the good works of the ASPCA became apparent, he gained respect. Bergh's supporters referred to him as an angel in a top hat.

This angel had a ubiquitous presence. Along with his agents, he walked the beat of New York City streets, alleys, and docks. He kept a copy of the new law in the pocket of his elegant frock coat. He also kept a watchful eye on slaughterhouse workers and butchers, sportsmen, drivers of carts and carriages, and others who might abuse animals.

Bergh described his routine to a reporter. "Day after day I am in slaughterhouses, or lying in wait at midnight with a squad of police near some dog pit. Lifting a fallen horse to his feet, penetrating buildings where I inspect collars and saddles for raw flesh, then lecturing in public schools to children, and again to adult societies. Thus my whole life is spent."

He was the whirlwind behind the evolving ASPCA. Bergh insisted on wearing multiple hats. Along with his roles as founder and president, he acted as administrator, animal caregiver, community advocate, diplomat, director of communications, educator, fundraiser, humane law enforcer, and lobbyist.

For his constant vigilance, Bergh earned his nickname, the Great Meddler. He wore it with pride.

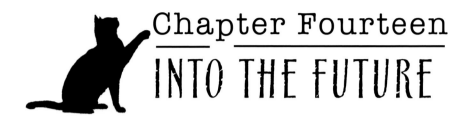

Chapter Fourteen
INTO THE FUTURE

H enry Bergh was an enigma.

For the first half-century of his life, Bergh displayed little interest in the plight of animals, yet he would launch the American Society for the Prevention of Cruelty to Animals — the first animal welfare organization in North America.

Although he never became a father or welcomed a pet into his family, Bergh dedicated his life to protecting children and animals. Although he claimed to be a carnivore out of habit while professing that bloody meat shocked his "sensibilities," Bergh preached the benefits of eliminating animal flesh from the diet. Although he championed the plight of horses, Bergh supported consuming horseflesh as a way to recycle old, lame carriage horses. Although he never hesitated to halt a dogfight, Bergh cringed when a curious canine offered a paw. Although he abhorred animal suffering of any kind, Bergh wore a winter coat and boots lined with fur and purchased an ermine cape and muff for his wife. And although he fearlessly faced his foes, in the privacy of his home Bergh wept for all the abused animals.

Bergh gave up his creature comforts to champion all creatures great and small. He had finally started earning respect for his compassion. *Scribner's Monthly* magazine proclaimed him a hometown hero in its 1879 issue: "It may almost be said of Henry Bergh that he has invented a new type of goodness, since invention is only the perception and application of truths that are eternal."

However, after twenty-two years of defending abused animals and prosecuting more than 12,000 cruelty cases, Bergh found his health declining. By the 1880s, he suffered from chronic bronchitis and enlargement of the heart.

Bergh's wife had died in 1887, and the widower shared quarters with two of his nephews in a Fifth Avenue brownstone. On March 11, during the Blizzard of Eighty-Eight, when a ferocious storm dumped twenty-one inches of snow and winds created snowdrifts up to twenty feet, the bedridden Bergh died in his home at the age of seventy-four.

Newspapers eulogized him. "The man who loved his fellow animal is mourned by his fellow man," the *New York Citizen* announced. The obituary continued, "So firm a hold did he take on the public sense of right that it is impossible that his work shall not be continued. He has made too many converts to render it [at] all likely that his commonwealth will ever relapse into a condition to witness cruelty to animals without resentment."

The *New York Times* agreed: "No greater monument can ever be erected to Henry Bergh than the fame of this society."

The *New York Post* reminded its readers, "His society was distinctly a one man power. The Society for the Prevention of Cruelty to Animals was Henry Bergh and Henry Bergh was the Society for the Prevention of Cruelty to Animals."

Despite snow so deep that it gripped the hubs of the hearse's wheels, many of Bergh's illustrious friends attended his funeral and burial in Brooklyn's Green-Wood Cemetery. His old nemesis turned friend, P. T. Barnum, served as one of the pallbearers. A poem about

Bergh written by his friend, the poet Henry Wadsworth Longfellow, was read:

> "*Among the noblest of the land;*
> *Though he may count himself the least;*
> *That man I honor and revere;*
> *Who, without favor, without fear;*
> *In the great city dares to stand;*
> *The friend of every friendless beast.*"

The social reformer and minister Henry Ward Beecher had previously written a tribute to Bergh, describing what would occur when Bergh entered Heaven. "Will there be no commotion among animals? The birds will tell it. The beasts of the field will know it. Even tropical turtles will feel briny tears. Airy elephants will bear him up; the spirits of released horses will prance about him; [cats] will purr celestial satisfaction, and rub his legs with their most beseeching caresses. Dogs without number ... will turn their great lustrous eyes upon him with refulgent gratitude. Yea, the whole air will be full of emancipated animals ... all tenderly eager to greet and honor the benefactor of animals."

Bergh had refused attempts to erect a statue in his

Newspapers eulogized Bergh: "The man who loved his fellow animal is mourned by his fellow man."

honor, telling his supporters that their "well-meant kindness would injure the cause." Finally, in 1891, a statue to the memory of Bergh was unveiled in Milwaukee, Wisconsin. James H. Mahoney created the bronze sculpture depicting the ASPCA founder dressed in a frock coat, holding a cane, and petting the head of a dog with a bandaged paw. The Wisconsin Humane Society raised $14,000 to erect the statue, which is the only Bergh statue in the country.

Also contrary to Bergh's wishes, the ASPCA took over animal control in 1894 by accepting a contract from New York City to run the dog pound. The society replaced the pound with animal shelters in New York City, followed by Brooklyn, and then Staten Island. The new shelters, according an 1895 edition of *Brooklyn's Sunday Advertiser*, were "conducted on kind and merciful principles."

The ASPCA responded to animal cruelty complaints for 147 years (until January 2014) from its New York headquarters on East Ninety-Second Street. Humane law enforcement agents wore uniforms, flashed badges, and carried handguns, pepper spray, batons, and handcuffs. They patrolled the city streets in blue and white squad cars.

The ASPCA's "animal cops" even starred on a reality TV show, *Animal Precinct*, which debuted in 2001. Viewers followed eighteen animal cruelty agents with full police powers as they investigated cruelty complaints in New York City — America's biggest metropolis, home to eight million people and five million animals.

However, in January 2014 the ASPCA laid off its agents. The New York Police Department (NYPD) took over responsibility for enforcing humane laws and responding to animal cruelty (the ASPCA would continue to provide support for animal cruelty victims). While the ASPCA maintained that the 34,000 police officers were better positioned to stay on top of complaints, critics argued that the NYPD would give crimes against animals a lower priority.

Today the national nonprofit charity is one of the largest animal welfare organizations in the world, with more than two million supporters. Its mission continues to be "to provide effective means for the prevention of cruelty to animals throughout the United States."

Bergh's dream to transform the ASPCA into a nationwide organization resulted in a network of similar state and municipal societies linking across America.

They extend what Bergh called the "humane and civilizing" benefits of the ASPCA. These societies might share the goal of prevention of cruelty to animals, but the ASPCA is not directly affiliated with any of these societies. Each society has its own policies, governing structure, and funding.

The ASPCA spends the biggest percentage of its budget on animal health services and public education programs. It adopts out cats and dogs from its state-of-the-art animal shelter in New York City, after spaying and neutering them to combat pet overpopulation. The Bergh Memorial Animal Hospital (now called the ASPCA Animal Hospital), which opened in 1912 in New York City, provides veterinary services for small animals. A mobile clinic also serves the area, altering and vaccinating pets, and a mobile adoption van matches shelter pets with potential adopters.

While a web of laws protects modern American animals, the ASPCA continues to wage many of the same battles against animal cruelty that Bergh did. It lobbies for stronger laws to protect horses, including the more than two hundred carriage horses who still toil citywide on Manhattan streets up to nine hours a day, seven days a week. It advocates against dogfighting, now an illegal underground blood "sport" that is a felony in all fifty states. It speaks out against forcing wild and exotic animals to perform in circuses. And it fights for stronger laws for farm animals raised for meat and milk.

The ASPCA encourages its supporters to visit the ASPCA website, where they, too, can advocate for animals. There, the next generation of animal lovers can learn how to get involved and make a difference for animals in their neighborhoods. And they can keep Henry Bergh's legacy alive by making our world a more humane place.

An engraved portrait of Henry Bergh proudly wearing his ASPCA president badge.

A historic map of Lower Manhattan.

A DOG FIGHT

Spectators jammed into a pit to bet on the winners of brutal dogfights.

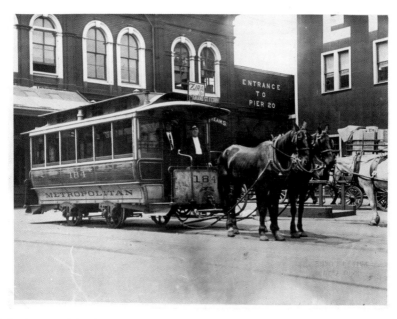

In 1832, the world's first horse-drawn street railway started up in New York.

A formal portrait of Henry Bergh.

Mary Ellen, at the time of her rescue on April 9, 1874.

Dogs in the kennels of a pound clamor for attention in 1899.

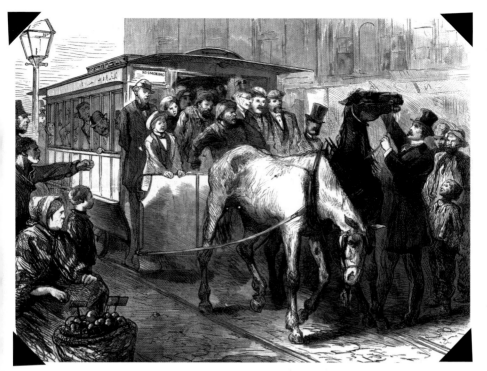

This engraving, which appeared in *Harper's Weekly* in September 1872, shows Bergh stopping an overcrowded streetcar that a pair of horses futilely strain to pull.

TURNSPIT.—*Canis vertagus.*

Turnspit dogs were bred to have long bodies and short, crooked front legs so they could run for hours inside a wheel that turned a roasting spit.

Clinton Hall

"The Brains," a Thomas Nast cartoon spoofing Boss Tweed, appeared in *Harper's Weekly* in October 1871.

THE "BRAINS"

This Thomas Nast woodcut entitled "Mr. Bergh to the Rescue" appeared in *Harper's Weekly* in August 1871.

This political cartoon, which appeared in *Puck,* insinuated that Bergh had empathy for animals but was insensitive to human suffering.

The Broadway entrance to Barnum's American Museum in 1858.

Phineas Taylor (P. T.) Barnum posed with "General" Tom Thumb circa 1850.

Jumbo and his trainer, Matthew Scott.

A team of horses pulls one of the last horse-drawn railcars along Broadway; electric trolleys gradually replaced horse-powered public transportation.

NEW YORK CITY.—NEW HEADQUARTERS OF THE AMERICAN SOCIETY FOR THE PREVENTION OF CRUELTY TO ANIMALS, FOURTH AVENUE AND TWENTY-SECOND STREET.—SEE PAGE 261.

The New York City headquarters of the American Society for the Prevention of Cruelty to Animals opened in 1876 at the corner of Fourth Avenue and Twenty-Second Street.

A NOTE FROM THE AUTHOR

I first encountered Henry Bergh when I discovered that my birthday — April 10 — coincided with the same day that the ASPCA was founded in 1866. Intrigued, I researched this mysterious New Yorker behind the first humane society in North America. Bergh quickly joined my list of zoological heroes, including Saint Francis of Assisi, Jeremy Bentham, Pete Singer, and Henry Spira.

It was time for Bergh's dynamic story to be written so the next generation of animal activists would be inspired into action. I spent years researching, writing, and revising. Along the way I discovered intriguing nuggets as my research diverged in a labyrinth of directions: what jobs turnspit dogs performed, why cows dispensed blue milk, how a political cartoon brought down Boss Tweed, what circus trick commanded President George Washington's attention — all of these and more helped humanize the history behind the ASPCA.

This book combines my dual passions: writing and animals. I started my writing career in third grade, when my class performed a play I had written while recovering from chicken pox. Since then, I've been a feature writer for a daily newspaper, a managing editor of trade and consumer magazines, and an editor at two children's book publishing houses. Now I'm a freelance writer, the best job in the world!

One of the reasons I write books is to support my menagerie. I've always adored animals. Life without them would be like living in black-and-white instead of color. Today my furry family includes big black dogs

and house rabbits — all rescued. I volunteer, rescue, transport, foster, and rehome pets for a variety of animal organizations. I chose to stop eating meat when I was sixteen. I've been speaking up for animals since I learned to talk, and I haven't shut up yet.

I hope readers will share my compassion for all creatures great and small, wild and domestic. You can be a hero to animals no matter what your age. Brainstorm creative ideas and use your dogged determination to make a difference. Remember that throughout history, the power of one ordinary person has changed the world in extraordinary ways.

Me and Jolly.

Me and Marshmallow.

TIMELINE

1813　August 29 — Henry Bergh is born in New York City.

1822　July 22 — The Ill-Treatment of Cattle Bill (Martin's Act) becomes the first animal-protection law in the world.

1824　The Society for the Prevention of Cruelty to Animals (SPCA) forms in London.

1830　Bergh enters Columbia College to study law.

1831–36　Bergh travels abroad in Europe.

1832　The world's first horse-drawn street railway starts up in New York.

1839　Bergh marries Catherine Matilda Taylor.

1859　Charles Darwin publishes *On the Origin of Species*.

1860　Abraham Lincoln is elected president.

1861–65　American Civil War

1863　Bergh is appointed to a diplomatic post at the Russian court of Czar Alexander II.

1865　Bergh meets with the Earl of Harrowby, president of the Royal Society for the Prevention of Cruelty to Animals.

1866 February 8—Bergh gives a lecture titled "Statistics Related to the Cruelties Practiced on Animals" at Clinton Hall.

April 10—The American Society for the Prevention of Cruelty to Animals (ASPCA) forms.

Bergh battles the scientific classification of turtles during the turtle trial.

1867 The ASPCA designs, builds, and operates the first ambulance for injured horses.

The *New York World* publishes snake controversy letters between Bergh and P. T. Barnum.

1874 December 15—Bergh launches the New York Society for the Prevention of Cruelty to Children, the world's first child protection agency.

1887 Catherine Matilda Bergh dies in Manhattan.

1888 March 11—Henry Bergh dies at age seventy-four in Manhattan.

Henry Bergh statue on the grounds of the Wisconsin Humane Society.

QUOTE SOURCES

INTRODUCTION

ix "250 decent people . . .": Chris Pomorski, "The Brutal Honesty of a
   Bloodsport Baron," *Narratively*, August 8, 2013, narrative.ly/not
   -afraid-of-a-fight/the-brutal-honesty-of-a-bloodsport-baron.
   "I was never especially interested . . .": *New York Mail and Express*,
   June 1884.

1. A PRIVILEGED CHILDHOOD

6 "honestest": Stephen Zawitowski, "Bergh, Henry," Learning to Give,
   learningtogive.org/papers/paper357.html

7 "I don't suppose . . .": Lane and Zawistowski, p. 2.

2. A SOUR NOTE

10 "rich and lazy": Loeper, p. 9.

11 "I'm not going back . . .": "Henry Bergh: The Elegant Fighter,"
   National Museum of Animals and Society, www.museumofanimals
   .org/#/henry-bergh/3984717.

11 "There is positively no merit . . .": Loeper, p. 12.

15 "About 25 horses and 8 bulls . . .": Shelman and Lazoritz, p. 29.

3. SEEDS OF CHANGE

16 "Oh, don't worry . . .": Pace, p. 18.

18 "It is better to abolish . . .": John Simkin, "Tsar Alexander II,"
   Spartacus Educational, February 2015, spartacus-educational.com
   /RUSalexander2.htm.

20   "Even though I could see . . .": Coren and Bartlett, p. 169.

21   "Tell that oaf . . .": "Henry Bergh: The Elegant Fighter."

21   "As I looked at his dark brown face . . .": Coren and Bartlett, p. 169.

23   "I made up my mind . . .": Lane and Zawistowski, p. 10.

23   "Mankind is served by animals . . .": Loeper, p. 15.

4. BERGH'S INSPIRATION

24   "fought many battles . . .": Pain, p. 68.

27   "Sir, an ox cannot hold a pistol!": Shevelow, p. 185.

28   "a blustering and blundering blockhead": "Humanity Dick," National Museum of Animals and Society, www.museumofanimals.org/# /humanitydick/3745671.

30   "Before undertaking this labor . . .": Lane and Zawistowski, p. 11.

30   "long cherished dream . . .": Gerald Carson, "The Great Meddler," *American Heritage* 19, no. 1 (December 1967), www.american heritage.com/content/great-meddler.

5. A VOICE FOR THE VOICELESS

31   "The undersigned, sensible of the cruelties . . .": *Johnson's New Universal Cyclopædia*, p. 1398.

36   "This is a matter purely of conscience . . .": Deborah Rudacille, "Development of Alternatives to Animal Use for Safety Testing and Hazard Assessment," *Horizon International*, October 1999, www .solutions-site.org/node/84.

36   "these mute servants of mankind": "The History of the ASPCA," ASPCA website, www.aspca.org/about-us/about-the-aspca/ history-aspca.

36   "seemed to receive their most ecstatic throb . . .": Animal Shelter.org, American Society for the Prevention of Cruelty to

Animals — ASPCA W. Coast, www.animalshelter.org/shelters
/American_Society_for_the_Prevention_of_Cruelty_to_
Animals_-_ASPCA_W_Coast_rId343_rS_pC.html.

37　"I protest in the name of heaven . . .": C. C. Buel, "Henry Bergh and
His Work," *Scribner's Monthly*, vol. 17, November 1878 to April
1879, p. 871.

38　"the establishment of a society kindred . . .": Carson, "The Great
Meddler."

39　"glittering roster of luminaries": Homans, p. 201.

39　"The social and political rank . . .": Carson, "The Great Meddler."

6. HORSE SENSE

42　"Age is a point . . .": Buel, "Henry Bergh and His Work," p. 876.

42　"Can't beat my own horse . . .": Carson, "The Great Meddler."

44　"that noble creature . . ." and "that generous and faithful servant . . .":
Ibid.

46　"Bergh makes himself ridiculous . . .": Loeper, pp. 34–35.

47　"small two-page paper . . .": "The Early History of Newspaper
Publishing in New York State," New York State Education
Department, May 2009, www.nysl.nysed.gov/nysnp/history.htm.

50　"I have often longed to ask . . .": Alcott, *Fairy Tales and Fantasy
Stories*, p. 228. "Rosa's Tale" is available at www.readbookonline.net
/readOnLine/11330.

50　"packed into cars like fish in barrels": Robert C. Kennedy, *New
York Street Railroad Cars — What We Are Coming To?*, HarpWeek
Cartoon of the Day, 2001, www.harpweek.com/09Cartoon/Related
Cartoon.asp?Month=March&Date=23.

51　"Never full! pack 'em in! . . .": Ibid.

51 "The horse, what does he get . . .": ASPCA Horse Protection History, www.aspca.org/get-involved/horses/aspca-horse-protection-history.

51 "dead horses and vehicular entanglements": Joel Tarr and Clay McShane, "The Centrality of the Horse to the Nineteenth-Century American City," *Enviroliteracy*, 1997, www.enviroliteracy.org/article. php/578.html.

52 "turn [her] brains into . . .": Alcott, p. 14.

52 "great rubbish": Cheney, p. 68.

53 "So I plod away . . .": Ibid., p. 199.

53 "moral pap . . ." and "the goose that laid . . .": *Louisa May Alcott: The Woman Behind* Little Women, film produced by Nancy Porter Productions, Inc., and Thirteen/WNET New York's American Masters, 2015, www.alcottfilm.com/louisa-may-alcott/life/literary-celebrity.

54 "The few dollars you might get . . .": Loeper, p. 38.

55 "great, lean, rawboned beasts": Lane and Zawistowski, p. 50.

55 "That ambulance preaches . . .": Buel, "Henry Bergh and His Work," p. 884.

7. TURTLES: ANIMALS OR INSECTS?

58 "If I had it my way . . .": Hoff, p. 29.

60 "To say that the turtle . . .": Pace, p. 47.

61 "Moses of the [animal rights] movement": Buel, "Henry Bergh and His Work," p. 880.

61 "I have always felt grateful . . .": Carson, "The Great Meddler."

61 "Having no desire to wound the feelings . . .": Pace, p. 45.

62 "not an animal . . .": "Henry Bergh's Story," *Philadelphia Press*, September 22, 1884.

62 "As for your gift . . .": Lane and Zawistowski, p. 129.

65 "If I were paid a large salary . . .": Buel, "Henry Bergh and His Work,"
    p. 875.

8. SWILL MILK AND SLAUGHTERHOUSES

69 "These foul prisons . . .": Loeper, p. 45.

70 "fatally poisoned 8,000 . . .": "How We Poison Our Children," *New
    York Times*, May 13, 1858, query.nytimes.com/mem/archive-free/
    pdf?res=F10913FB3E581B7493C1A8178ED85F4C8584F9.

71 "It took heroism . . .": Loeper, p. 46.

71 "by basely counterfeiting . . .": "A Lecture by Henry Bergh: He Tells
    the Farmers' Club What He Knows about Milk and Swill Milk,"
    New York Times, March 27, 1878, query.nytimes.com/mem/archive
    -free/pdf?res=F30D15FD3F5A127B93C5AB1788D85F4C8784F9.

71 "Now, is it not to be supposed . . .": Henry Bergh, "The Cost of
    Cruelty," *North American Review*, vol. 133, July 1, 1881.

73 "cannot be suppressed . . .": Ibid.

75 "Remember, the same starlit . . .": Loeper, p. 40.

75 "How can you sleep . . .": Ibid., p. 39.

75 "The laws of God and man . . .": Zulma Steele, "Friend of the
    Friendless Animals," in New Radiant Readers, Book 10, p. 107.

76 "put a stop to these hellish practices": Loeper, p. 41.

9. COMPASSION FOR CANINES

78 "Look at the spit dog": Davia Nelson and Nikki Silva, "Turnspit
    Dogs: The Rise and Fall of the Vernepator Cur," *NPR Blog*, May 13,
    2014, www.npr.org/blogs/thesalt/2014/05/13/311127237
    /turnspit-dogs-the-rise-and-fall-of-the-vernepator-cur.

80 "modified for different ends": Matt Ridley, "Modern Darwins,"

National Geographic, February 2009, ngm.nationalgeographic.com
/print/2009/02/darwin-legacy/ridley-text.

84 "The underside of . . .": Coren and Bartlett, p. 171.

84 "could not see how it was . . .": Ibid., p. 172.

85 "A sport should not be the enjoyment": Loeper, pp. 53–54.

85 "the civilization of a people . . .": Joan M. Bundy, "Animal Cruelty and Neglect: Detecting, Investigating and Reporting Suspected Animal Abuse and Understanding Its Connection to Other Crimes," Slideshare, April 30, 2010, www.slideshare.net/ShoneyB/animal -cruelty-presentation-for-officers.

87 "The rapidity with which . . .": Pomorski, "The Brutal Honesty of a Bloodsport Baron."

89 "maliciously kill, maim, wound . . .": "Rats II: Man vs. Vermin," *History House*, www.historyhouse.com/in_history/rats_2.

89 "simply sickening" and "surrounded by a crowd . . .": David W. Dunlap, "A Scruffy Old Tavern Is Now Luxury Apartments," *New York Times*, October 27, 1998, www.nytimes.com/1998/10/27 /nyregion/a-scruffy-old-tavern-is-now-luxury-apartments .html?pagewanted=2&src=pm.

92 "a mass of blood, her jaws . . .": Loeper, p. 52.

92 "Your society is doing a noble work, sir . . .": Carson, "The Great Meddler."

93 "The canine species . . .": Coren and Bartlett, p. 258.

94 "in a manner greatly detrimental . . .": "The History of the ASPCA," ASPCA website, www.aspca.org/about-us/about-the-aspca/ history-aspca.

94 "It does not necessarily follow . . .": Buel, "Henry Bergh and His Work," p. 880.

96   "that the wholesale slaughter . . .": Henry Bergh, "Mr. Bergh and the Dogs," *New York Times*, September 25, 1868, davideharrington .com/wp-content/uploads/2013/01/Mr-Bergh-and-the-Dogs.pdf.

96   "the arresting officer . . .": Coren and Bartlett, p. 258.

97   "A large crate, seven feet long . . .": "Destroying the Dogs," *New York Times*, July 6, 1877, cityroom.blogs.nytimes.com/2008/09/30 /where-they-used-to-drown-the-dogs.

98   "some good-sized animals" and "instantaneous and merciful death": Daly, p. 200.

98   "To me there is always . . .": Loeper, p. 70.

100 "This Society could not stultify . . .": Winograd, p. 11.

10. "CIVILIZED" BLOOD SPORTS

104 "Dog hunting and water . . .": Loeper, p. 70.

104 "Figs do not grow . . .": Buel, "Henry Bergh and His Work," p. 882.

105 "Then why not man . . .": Loeper, p. 70.

105 "cruel and unmanly sport": Henry Bergh, "Pigeon Shooting," *New York Times*, December 31, 1871.

105 "capable of deriving pleasure . . .": Ibid.

107 "There seems to be an appetite . . .": George A. Gipe, "The Sensation Promised New York in 1880 Was a Lot More Bull Than Fight," *Sports Illustrated*, July 19, 1976, www.si.com /vault/1976/07/19/615908/the-sensation-promised-new-york -in-1880-was-a-lot-more-bull-than-fight.

107 "Driving a frightened steer . . .": Ibid.

11. BATTLING BARNUM

108 "daring & dangerous . . .": "Barnum and Bailey Greatest Show on Earth Daring and Dangerous Equestrian Act" poster, circa 1898,

reproduction number LC-USZC4–10495, Library of Congress Prints and Photographs Division, www.loc.gov/pictures /item/2002735827.

109 "an act of cruelty and terror": Loeper, p. 76.

109 "simply abominable that the public . . .": Barnum, p. 236.

109 "I shall place a hoop of fire . . .": Carson, "The Great Meddler."

109 "vaulted about with . . .": Fleming, p. 127.

111 "patron saint of promoters": "P. T. Barnum," Ringling Bros. and Barnum & Bailey website, www.ringling.com/FlashSubContent .aspx?id=11734&parentID=366&assetFolderID=368.

111 "amusement which consists . . .": Loeper, p. 74.

112 "evil corrected": "Letters Between P. T. Barnum and Henry Bergh of the ASPCA," Roy Rosenzweig Center for History and New Media, George Mason University, chnm.gmu.edu/ lostmuseum/lm/192.

112 "protesting against the cruel mode . . .": Ibid.

112 "Any person who can commit . . .": Ibid.

112 "Your arbitrary conduct . . .": Ibid.

112 "I do not think the most active member . . .": Ibid.

113 "It may be urged that these reptiles . . .": Ibid.

113 "low breeding and a surplus of self-conceit": Rivas, p. 88.

113 "The snake controversy . . .": "Letters Between P. T. Barnum and Henry Bergh of the ASPCA."

113 "incarcerating poor helpless dumb . . .": Loeper, p. 74.

114 "Speaking, Sir, of inhumanity": "Letters Between P. T. Barnum and Henry Bergh of the ASPCA."

117 "It is a fact that he is . . .": P. T. Barnum interview, *Philadelphia Press*, April 22, 1882.

118 "honored and respected . . .": Barnum, *Selected Letters*, p. 254.

118 "one of the most humane . . .": Barnum, *The King of the Animal Kingdom*, p. 279.

12. COMPASSION FOR CHILDREN

121 "only a piece of carpet . . .": "Mary Ellen's Court Statement," New York Society for the Prevention of Cruelty to Children, www.nyspcc .org/about/history.

121 "I have no recollection . . .": Ibid.

121 "I do not want to go back . . .": Ibid.

124 "The children of New York . . .": Ibid.

124 "It is not alone . . .": Ibid.

124 "Is there anything more helpless . . .": Coren and Bartlett, pp. 176–77.

125 "Men will be just . . .": Ibid., p. 173.

125 "He wanders the landscape . . .": Coren, p. 177.

125 "The child is an animal . . .": Coren and Bartlett, p. 178.

126 "I regard a helpless child . . .": Shelman and Lazoritz, *Out of the Darkness*, p. 251.

13. THE GREAT MEDDLER

129 "Stop them damn pictures . . .": Navasky, p. 79.

130 "an ass that should have . . .": Carson, "The Great Meddler."

130 "Cockroaches . . . insist on sharing the best . . .": Ibid.

130–31 "furious opposition . . . ," "the better classes . . . ," "a snapping, snarling crowd . . .": Van Benschoten, p. 670.

132 "I fear neither disease . . .": Loeper, pp. 27–28.

132 "jolly good cry": Buel, "Henry Bergh and His Work," p. 881.

133 "Two or three years . . .": Winograd, p. 187.

133 "I have adopted a habit . . .": Carson, "The Great Meddler."

134 "to plant, or revive . . .": Ibid.

134 "Day after day I am in slaughterhouses . . .": "The History of the ASPCA."

14. INTO THE FUTURE

137 "It may almost be said . . .": Buel, "Henry Bergh and His Work," p. 872.

138 "The man who loved . . .": Carson, "The Great Meddler."

138 "So firm a hold . . .": "The History of the ASPCA."

138 "No greater monument . . .": "Death of Henry Bergh," *New York Times*, March 13, 1888, query.nytimes.com/mem/archive-free/pdf?r es=9F02E6D8173AE033A25750C1A9659C94699FD7CF.

138 "His society was distinctly . . .": Winograd, p. 13.

139 "Among the noblest of the land . . .": Nathan Winograd, "Top 2010 No-Kill Advocates Honored," *Examiner*, December 12, 2010, www .examiner.com/article/top-2010-no-kill-advocates-honored.

139 "Will there be no commotion among the animals? . . ." Henry Ward Beecher, "All Hail to Henry Bergh," *Christian Union*, vol. 7, no. 4, January 22, 1873.

141 "well-meant kindness": Buel, "Henry Bergh and His Work," p. 876.

141 "conducted on kind and merciful": Coren and Bartlett, p. 258.

142 "to provide effective means . . .": "Mission," ASPCA website, www .aspca.org/about-us/aspca-policy-and-position-statements/mission.

143 "humane and civilizing": Lane and Zawistowski, p. 142.

★★★ BIBLIOGRAPHY ★★★

Alcott, Louisa May. *The Selected Letters of Louisa May Alcott.* Edited by Joel Myerson, Daniel Shealy, and Madeleine B. Stern. Athens: University of Georgia Press, 1995.

———. *Fairy Tales and Fantasy Stories.* Edited by Daniel Shealy. Knoxville: University of Tennessee Press, 1992.

Barnum, P. T. *The King of the Animal Kingdom; How He Caught, Tamed and Ruled His Subjects; Natural History from a New Standpoint.* Chicago: R. S. Peale, 1889.

———. *Selected Letters of P. T. Barnum.* Edited by A. H. Saxon. New York: Columbia University Press, 1983.

Bekoff, Marc. *Encyclopedia of Animal Rights and Animal Welfare.* Westport, CT: Greenwood Press, 1998.

Bial, Raymond. *Rescuing Rover: Saving America's Dogs.* New York: Houghton Mifflin Harcourt, 2011.

Cheney, Ednah Dow, editor. *Louisa May Alcott: Her Life, Letters, and Journals.* Carlisle, MA: Applewood Books (reprint edition), 2010.

Coren, Stanley. *Why We Love Dogs the Way We Do.* New York: Fireside, 1998.

Coren, Stanley, and Andy Bartlett. *The Pawprints of History: Dogs and the Course of Human Events.* New York: Free Press, 2002.

Daly, Michael. *Topsy: The Startling Story of the Crooked-Tailed Elephant, P. T. Barnum, and the American Wizard, Thomas Edison.* New York: Atlantic Monthly Press, 2013.

Fleming, Candace. *The Great and Only Barnum: The Tremendous, Stupendous Life of Showman P. T. Barnum.* New York: Schwartz and Wade, 2009.

Hoff, Syd. *The Man Who Loved Animals*. New York: Coward, McCann and Geoghegan, 1982.

Homans, John. *What's a Dog For? The Surprising History, Science, Philosophy, and Politics of Man's Best Friend*. New York: Penguin Press, 2012.

Johnson's New Universal Cyclopædia: A Scientific and Popular Treasury of Useful Knowledge. New York: Alvin J. Johnson & Son. 1877.

Lane, Marion, and Stephen L. Zawistowski. *Heritage of Care: the American Society for the Prevention of Cruelty to Animals*. Westport, CT: Praeger, 2008.

Loeper, John J. *Crusade for Kindness: Henry Bergh and the ASPCA*. New York: Atheneum, 1991.

Miller-Schroeder, Patricia. *The ASPCA*. Mankato, MN: Weigl, 2003.

Navasky, Victor S. *The Art of Controversy: Political Cartoons and Their Enduring Power*. New York: Alfred A. Knopf, 2013.

Pace, Mildred Mastin. *Friend of Animals: The Story of Henry Bergh*. New York: C. Scribner's Sons, 1942.

Pain, Wellesley. *Richard Martin*. Whitefish, MT: Kessinger Publishing, LLC, 2003.

Phillips, Peter. *Humanity Dick: The Eccentric Member for Galway*. London: Parapress, 2003.

Rivas, Mim Eichler. *The Lost History of a Horse and a Man Who Changed the World*. New York: HarperCollins, 2005.

Sante, Luc. *Low Life: Lures and Snares of Old New York*. New York: Vintage, 1992.

Shelman, Eric A., and Stephen Lazoritz. *The Mary Ellen Wilson Child Abuse Case and the Beginning of Children's Rights in Nineteenth-Century America*. Jefferson, NC: McFarland, 2005.

———. *Out of the Darkness, The Story of Mary Ellen Wilson*. Cape Coral, FL: Dolphin Moon Publishing, 1999.

Shevawn, Lynam. *Humanity Dick. A Biography of Richard Martin*. London: Hamish Hamilton, 1975.

Shevelow, Kathryn. *For the Love of Animals: The Rise of the Animal Protection Movement*. New York: Henry Holt, 2008.

Suen, Anastasia. *ASPCA: The American Society for the Prevention of Cruelty to Animals*. New York: Rosen Publishing Group's Powerkids, 2002.

Van Benschoten, William Henry. *Concerning the Van Benschoten or Van Bunschoten Family in America*. Poughkeepsie, NY: A.V. Haight Co., 1907.

Winograd, Nathan J. *Redemption: The Myth of Pet Overpopulation and the No-Kill Revolution in America*. San Clemente, CA: Almaden Books, 2007.

You can learn more about the history of the American Society for the Prevention of Cruelty to Animals at their website: www.aspca.org. There you can also discover ways to make a difference for animals today.

PICTURE CREDITS

INDEX

Note: Page references in *italics* indicate photographs and their captions.

A

Agassiz, Louis, 60, 112–13
Alcott, Louisa May, 50, 52–53
Alexander II, emperor of Russia, 18
ambulances, for horses, 55, 65
American Museum, 111–15, *152*
animal kingdom, 63
Animal Precinct (TV show), 142
animals
    humane treatment, concept of, xiii–xiv
    lack of empathy toward, 27–28
    shelters for, 94–100, 141, *148*
animal welfare societies, 25. *See also* ASPCA
ASPCA (American Society for the Prevention of Cruelty to Animals)
    Animal Hospital, 143
    Bergh's many roles at, 135
    budget, 143
    on "civilized" blood sports, 104
    conviction success rates, 62
    donations from children, 62–64
    first anti-cruelty bill, 39–40
    first conviction, 43
    first major donor, 64
    growth in membership, 62
    headquarters, 64–65, 141, *153*
    incorporation, 39
    investigative agents, 65–66, 142
    lobbying efforts, 143–44
    mission, 142
    nationwide, 142–44
    P. T. Barnum's gift to, 119
    staff, 65
    takes over city dog pound, 141
Astley, Philip, 116
Astor, John Jacob, Jr., 34, 38
Atlantic Monthly, 51

B

Bailey, James A., 117
Barnum, P. T., *152*
    attends Bergh's funeral, 138
    circus of, 108–9, 116, 117
    friendship with Bergh, 118–19
    museum of, 111–15, *152*
    snake controversy, 111–13
Barnum & Bailey's circus, 117
bear fights, 88
Beecher, Henry Ward, 139
Bellevue Hospital, 55
Bennett, James Gordon, 100
Bergh, Catherine, 11–12, 132, 137
Bergh, Christian, 5–6, 7, 12
Bergh, Elizabeth, 6–7
Bergh, Henry, *146*, *148*
    birth, 2
    cartoons depicting, 127, 130, *151*
    childhood, 7–9
    college years, 10–11

commits to animal rights
movement, 23
courage and physical strength,
66
critics of, 127–33
death, 137–38
declining health, 137
enigmatic nature, 136–37
eulogies about, 138
European travels, 11, 12–15
fights for children's rights,
125–26
friendship with P. T. Barnum,
118–19
funeral and burial, 138–39
inheritance, 12
joins shipbuilding business, 11
law enforcement duties, 134–35
lecture on animal protection,
31–38
marries Catherine Taylor,
11–12
nickname, 30
political career, 17–23
public respect for, 134
response to ridicule, 132–33
Russian diplomatic post, 17–23
sense of humor, 50
sensitive nature, 7
special connection to horses, 43
speeches about animal
protection, 133–34
statues honoring, 119, 141
threats against, 132
tribute to, 139
witnesses first bullfight, 13

writes about animal protection,
133
writing aspirations, 11, 12,
16–17
Bergh & Co., 11
Bergh Memorial Animal Hospital,
143
the Bible, 27–28, 81
blood sports, 36
boa constrictors, 111–13
Bonard, Louis, 64–65
Boss Tweed, 129, 150
bovine tuberculosis, 69
breed-specific legislation (BSL), 91
Brevoort, Henry, 7
Brooklyn's Sunday Advertiser, 141
bulldogs, 90
bullfighting, 13–15, 36, 106–7
Burns, Christopher "Kit," 87, 89, 92
Burr, Aaron, 48

C
Calhoun, Nehemiah, 57
canine bath tub, 97
caricature, 128–29
carriage horses, 20–21, 143
cartoons, political, 127–30, 150–
51
cats, 96, 98, 99
cattle
Ill-Treatment of Cattle Bill,
25–27
inhumane treatment of, 42–43,
71–75
Chamber of Horrors, 65
chickens, slaughtering of, 76

child labor laws, 83, 122
children
first child protection agency, 126
as laborers, 83, 122–23
mistreatment and exploitation
of, 83, 121–23
circus
history of, 116–17
performances, 108–9, 115–19
protecting animals at, 144
Cirque de Soleil, 117
city pounds, 94–100, 141, *148*
Clay, Cassius Marcellus, 17
clay pigeons, 106
cockfighting, 36, 93
Columbia College, 10–11
Cooper, Peter, 34, 38
cows, dairy, 67–71

D
dairy industry
deplorable conditions, 67–70
health investigations, 70–71
overhaul of, 71
poor quality feed, 67–69
stronger laws for, 144
Darwin, Charles, 77–78, 79–81
Declaration of the Rights of
Animals, 34–35, 38
deer hunting, 104
Dickinson, Emily, 48
dogcatchers, 94, 97
dogfighting, *147*
dogs against bears, 88
dogs against monkeys, 24–25
dogs against rats, 87–88

investigations into, 65
made illegal, 89, 93
in New York City, x–xiii
opposition to, 85, 144
dogs
deer hunting and, 104
in early 1800s, 2
fox hunting and, 104
hare coursing and, 104
licensing of, 96
pit bulls, 90–91
stray, 93–100
turnspit, 2, 77–84, *149*
used to guard coaches, 85
used to pull carts, 85
drinking fountains, 56

E
Earl of Harrowby, 30, 38–39
Edison, Thomas Alva, 98
elephants, 115, 117, 119, *152*
Emancipation Manifesto, 18–19
Emancipation Proclamation, 19
Emerson, Ralph Waldo, 52
euthanasia, 98–99
Evening Post, 113
evolution, theory of, 79–81

F
Fair Labor Standards Act, 83, 122
Farmers' Club, 71
foie gras, 37
For the More Effectual Prevention
of Cruelty to Animals
(law), 39–40
fox hunting, 104

Frank Leslie's Illustrated Newspaper, 70

Franklin, Benjamin, 128

G

geese, 37

George IV, King of England, 25

Gerry, Elbridge T., 126

Great Britain, 24–29

Greeley, Horace, 35, 38

gyropigeon, 106

H

hare coursing, 104

Harper, Fletcher, 35, 38

Harper's Weekly, 50, 128, *150, 151*

Hartfield, T. W., 102, 108, 109

Hoffman, John T., 32, 35, 38

horses

    ambulances for, 55, 65

    death from plague, 54

    drinking troughs for, 56

    in New York City, 1, 43–56

    pulling carriages, 20–21, 143

    pulling carts, 41–42

    pulling streetcars, 1, 44–51, *147, 149, 153*

    rescuing, with canvas sling, 55–56

    retirement stables for, 55

Hospital Sketches (Alcott), 52

I

Ill-Treatment of Cattle Bill, 25–27

Irving, Washington, 48

Ivers, Elizabeth, 6

J

Jacco Maccacco, 24–25

L

Life magazine, 111

Lincoln, Abraham, 17, 19, 30

Linnaeus, Carl, 63

Little Women (Alcott), 52–53

Longfellow, Henry Wadsworth, 139

M

Mahoney, James H., 141

Martin, Richard "Humanity Dick," 25–29, 30, 130

Martin's Act, 25–27, 29

Mary Ellen (orphan), 120–21, 123, 126, *148*

McCloskey, John, 32, 35

McClure's Magazine, 130–32

Melville, Herman, 48

Moore, Clement Clarke, 48

N

Nast, Thomas, 127–29, *150, 151*

natural selection, 80–81

navy ships, 5–6

newspapers

    criticize Bergh, 130

    in New York City, 47–49

New York Citizen, 138

New York City

    animal mortality rates, 72

child labor in, 83
drowning dogs in, 97
euthanasia rates in, 99
historical map of, 146
newspapers in, 47–49
police department, 142
sanitary conditions, 72
treatment of horses in, 43–56
New York Evening Telegram, 123
New-York Gazette, 47
New York Herald, 48–49, 61, 100, 107
New York Post, 138
New York Society for the Prevention of Cruelty to Children, 126
New York Sunday Mercury, 130
New York Times, 49, 70, 105, 138
New York Tribune, 49
New York World, 113
Nicholas I, Emperor of Russia, 18
no-kill policies, 99
Northern Budget of Troy, 123

O
On the Origin of Species (Darwin), 80

P
Pennsylvania Gazette, 128
pigeon shooting, 101–6, 105–6
pit bulls, 90–91
political cartoons, 127–30, 150–51
pounds, city, 94–100, 141, 148
public health practices, 72

R
rabies, 93, 95–96
railways and shipping companies, 71–74
rat fights, 87–88
Ricketts, John Bill, 116–17
Ringling Bros. circus, 117
Roosevelt, James J., 34, 38
Royal Society for the Prevention of Cruelty to Animals (RSPCA), 25, 29
Russia
Bergh's diplomatic post in, 17–23
carriage horses in, 20–21
under czar leadership, 18–19

S
Salamander the Fire Horse, 108–9
Schaack, Cornelius Van, 34, 38
Scribner's Monthly, 65, 137
Seward, William H., 17
Shattuck, Lemuel, 72
shelters, animal, 94–100, 141, 148
slaughterhouses, 42–43, 71–76
slavery, 17, 19
Smith, Stephen, 72
snakes, 111–13
Society for the Prevention of Cruelty to Animals (SPCA), 29. *See also* ASPCA
Society for the Prevention of Cruelty to Children, 126
sodium pentobarbital, 99

Sportsmen's Hall, x–xiii, 87, 89, 92
Stewart, Alexander T., 32, 34
stray dogs, 93–100
streetcars, horse-drawn, 1, 44–51,
    147, 149, 153
Struggles and Triumphs (Barnum),
    119
the *Sun*, 48
swill milk, 67–71

T
Taylor, Catherine Matilda, 11–12
Thirteenth Amendment of the U.S.
    Constitution, 19
Thoreau, Henry David, 52
trapshooting, 106
Tuomey, Michael, 70
turnspit dogs, 2, 77–84, *149*
turtles, green sea, 57–62
Twain, Mark, 48
Tweed, William Magear "Boss,"
    129, *150*

U
Unitarianism, 53

V
Victoria, Queen of England, 29
vivisection, 37

W
Washington, George, 93, 117
Wesley, James, John, and Joseph,
    35, 38
Wheeler, Etta, 123–25, 126
Whitman, Walt, 48
Wisconsin Humane Society, 141